INTEGRATED PRACT ON THE FRONT LINE

a Handbook

Written by Liz Garrett and Sal Lodge

Working with two Change Project groups

research in practice 2009

Tools These exercises and checklists will help you put some of the messages from the research into integrated working on the front line into practice. There are 14 Tools in all. All the Tools (and a list of their titles) are at the back of this Handbook. They are also provided as PDF files on the accompanying videoCD.

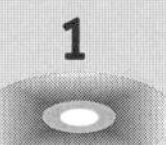

VideoCD The Handbook is accompanied by a videoCD. In a series of six short films, the people who worked with us to produce the materials share their learning and insights about what makes for effective integrated working on the front line. This videoCD stands alone and can be used independently of the Handbook. However, it works best if you use it to complement the written materials. Most sections of the Handbook have a related film on the videoCD, and this symbol will point you to the right track.

Case Examples These examples have been generated by the people who worked with us to produce this Handbook. They give you real, practical illustrations of how others have used the Tools or applied their learning about integrated practice.

Practical things you can do These are suggestions made by participants in the two Change Project groups – drawing on their expertise and experience.

What it feels like These are quotes from the people who worked with us to produce this Handbook. Here they share their experience and learning about the particular issues that surfaced during the life of the Change Project group meetings.

Top
Research
Tips

Top Research Tips These bite-size summaries at the end of some sections capture what the research told us about what was useful in terms of integrated practice. Research Tips are the things that teams must have in place in order for integrated working to be successful. They point to things to look out for and to avoid as well as 'tips' to develop and improve integrated practice.

Dig Deeper This is where you can see details about useful, relevant further information and resources. It will signpost you to relevant pages on our own or other websites, and direct you to useful publications and articles.

contents

Introduction

The story of the Change Project

This Handbook is the result of a Change Project that ran over a period of three years.

The process

The project had three phases. The first was a development group, which consisted of three representatives from five services engaged in integrated practice. In each case, the representatives came from different professional backgrounds and included a manager and two front-line practitioners.

The group met six times over a year to exchange their knowledge and experience in a structured and collaborative way. The structure was framed around the research discussed below. (Professor Nick Frost contributed to these sessions.)

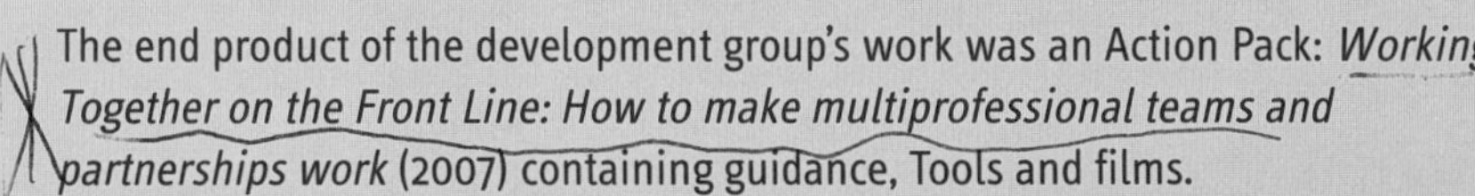

The end product of the development group's work was an Action Pack: *Working Together on the Front Line: How to make multiprofessional teams and partnerships work* (2007) containing guidance, Tools and films.

The Action Pack was then piloted with a second group of professionals, spanning a range of examples of integrated practice. The purpose of the pilot was to ensure the pack was accurate, relevant and easy to understand. Participants used the materials and reported back to the group on a) how they had used them b) whether they had had an impact on their existing integrated working and c) how the materials could be improved. Using this feedback, the Action Pack was adapted and rewritten into a Handbook.

The draft Handbook was then circulated to critical readers and revised accordingly. This final Handbook again consists of guidance, practical Tools and films.

The research background

We started by considering Nick Frost's research review *Professionalism, Partnership and Joined up Thinking: A research review of front-line working with children and families,* (2005) commissioned by **research in practice.** His review focused on what happens day to day when professionals work together. It was based on research and commentary in the field and drew on many examples of joined-up working across different professions and agencies. This review substantially shaped the work undertaken in the first development group. We used the research messages from the review to design the programme for that group and developed Tools using 'Research Tips' that he compiled to reflect the messages from the research.

As the group development work in the Change Project progressed, *Developing Multiprofessional Teamwork for Integrated Children's Services* was published in 2006 – a study by Angela Anning, David Cottrell, Nick Frost, Josephine Green and Mark Robinson. The purpose of the study was to try to understand how multiagency teams make integrated practice a reality and to look at some of the implications of this work.

The research messages in this study were distilled into an audit tool that identifies four themes or 'domains'. The second Change Project group felt these domains and the detail of the audit tool provided an accessible and clear framework to communicate the main research messages and assist practitioners and their managers to implement them. We therefore revisited the design of some of the Tools to accommodate the work of Anning et al.

Throughout, we have relied heavily on these two resources as they had translated research evidence into messages for practice and identified significant themes across those messages to help practitioners to use them.

During the period of development of this Handbook, the policy context and the language have continued to develop and change and more research has become available. (Carpenter and Dickinson, 2008; Daniels et al, 2008; Glasby and Dickinson, 2008) We have updated this version to accommodate more recent research and address the current picture of integrated practice.

Importantly, much of the content of this Handbook uses the group participants' voices and experience, married with the research to produce guidance that is based on the experience of practitioners on the front line as well as being research-informed.

A note about the terms we have used

We have moved through a spectrum of terms in the process of developing this work, trying to keep pace with the current terminology and policy directives over the period: 'joined-up' working, 'multiagency' teams, 'interprofessional' teams, 'partnerships' and, at the time of writing, 'integrated practice' and 'integrated teams'.

What do we mean by 'integrated working'?

The term integrated working is now widely used and understood, but the research and commentary covering the years 2000 to today use a range of different terms reflecting the journey to that common understanding. Anning et al acknowledge that confusion:

> *Between 2000 and 2006 confusion arose as the terms to describe joined-up working proliferated.*

In 2006, when we began this project, the Every Child Matters website suggested multiagency services could be classified using three broad models:

1. *A **multiagency panel** may deliver one task as a team – eg the allocation of referrals to the appropriate service, or the allocation of a pooled or aligned budget or service (such as respite breaks for disabled children)*
2. *Alternatively, some **multiagency teams** will come together for all (or the larger part) of a service, but typically not be a fully integrated service. So they will co-ordinate their work to a shared objective by joint working but remain employed by separate organisations*

3. *A* ***fully integrated team*** *will be made up of a range of practitioners 'seconded' from their separate agencies for an agreed period into the management of a single organisation or employed by one organisation.*

(Every Child Matters website)

In the intervening period a more complex picture has developed, responding to the need to create the potential for working together within and across teams and services, whether or not there are new structures.

The diagram, which shows how this works in one authority, captures that complexity. It also shows how one authority links its delivery structures to the Children's Trust partnership.

Processes such as the Common Assessment Framework (CAF), Lead Professional and information sharing agreements and protocols are as important as changed structures in supporting the formation of a 'virtual team' or 'team around the child' (TAC).

We have tried to make this Handbook useful to anyone involved in integrated working, by using inclusive terminology and presenting the work in a way that allows you to translate its messages to the range of models and circumstances in which integrated practice occurs.

Integrated working in Telford and Wrekin (2008)

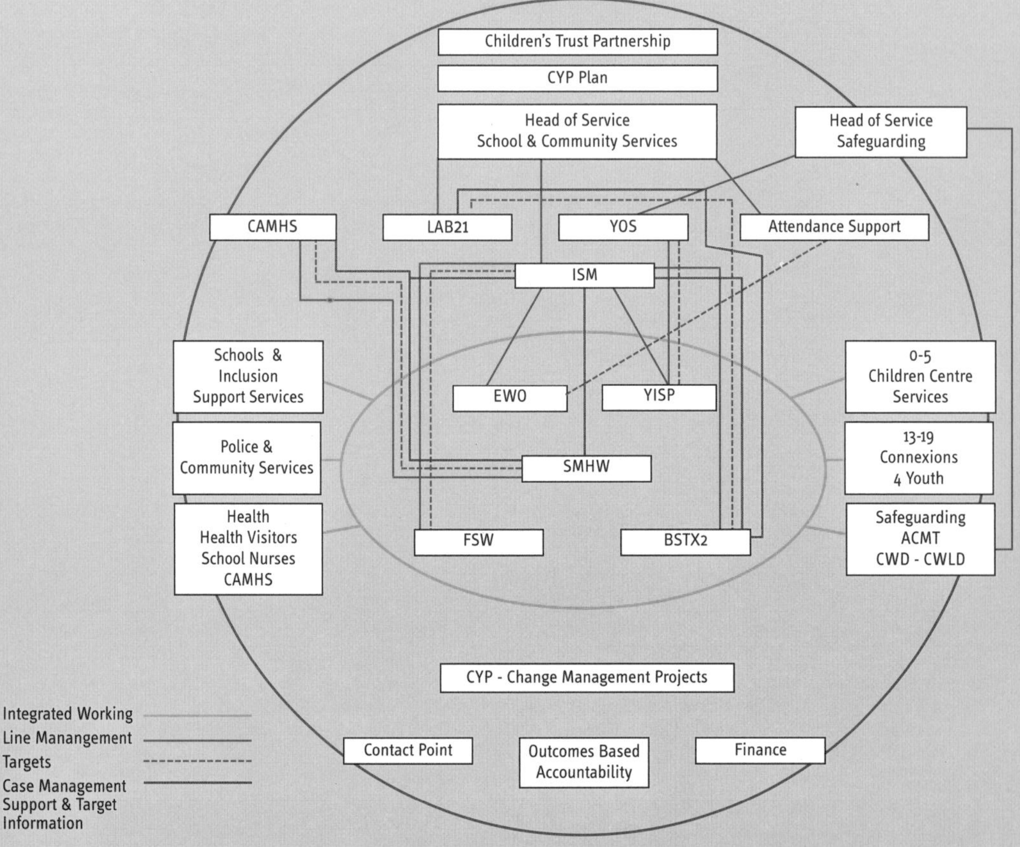

1

The policy context and supporting guidance

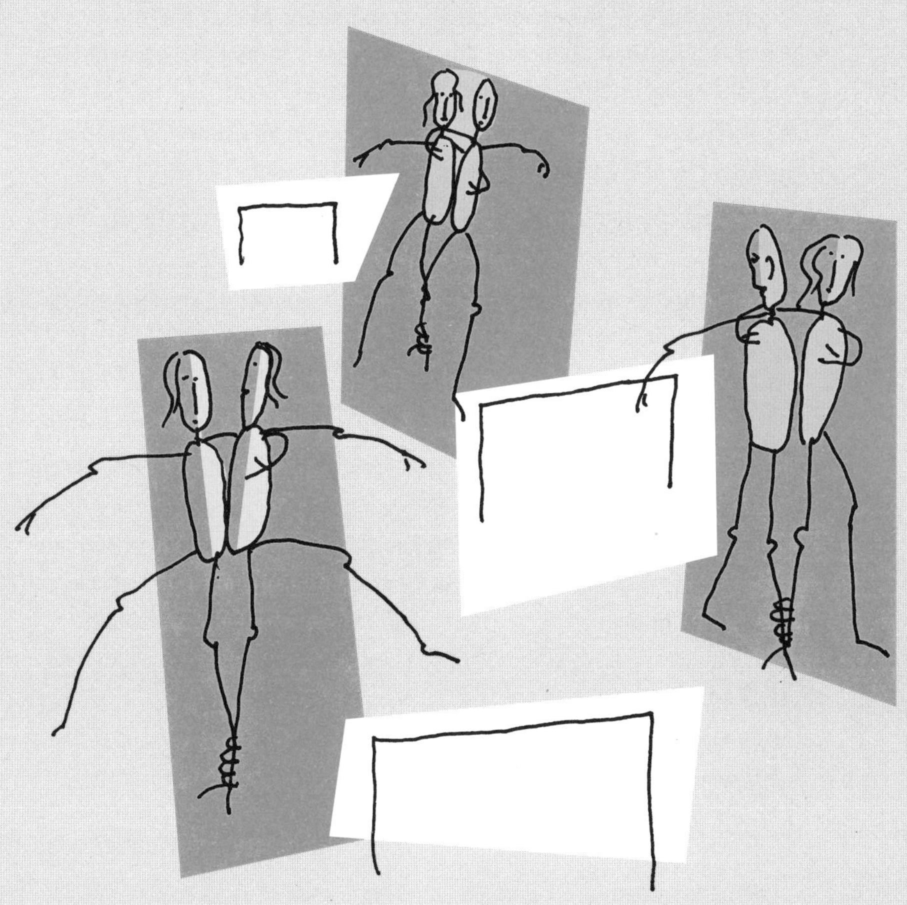

The policy context and supporting guidance

This chapter sets out the policy context and background to integrated working and describes the support provided by government agencies for this agenda.

Responding to a child's death: Every Child Matters

The call for professionals to work together more effectively on the front line emerged strongly in the government's green paper *Every Child Matters* (2003), which was published alongside the government's formal response to Lord Laming's inquiry into the tragic death of Victoria Climbié.

The green paper built on existing plans to strengthen children's services by focusing on four key themes:

- increasing the focus on supporting families and carers as the most critical influence on children's lives
- ensuring necessary intervention takes place before children reach crisis point, and protecting children from falling through the net
- addressing the underlying problems identified in the report into the death of Victoria Climbié – ie weak accountability and poor integration
- and ensuring that those who work with children are valued, rewarded and trained.

The failure of services to act on early warning signs or to build a complete picture was identified in the Victoria Climbié inquiry and others as a key failing. Lord Laming concluded that integrating professionals through multidisciplinary teams was one of the key developments that could overcome that failing.

> *Multiagency working has been shown to be an effective way of supporting children and young people with additional needs and securing real improvements in their life outcomes.*
>
> (Every Child Matters website)

DIG DEEPER for a list of key documents that explain and shape the strategic direction of the Every Child Matters: Change for Children programme.

Green paper *Every Child Matters* (2003) http://www.everychildmatters.gov.uk/publications/

The Victoria Climbié Inquiry (2003) www.victoria-climbie-inquiry.org.uk/finreport/finreport.htm

Every Child Matters: The next steps (2004) www.dcsf.gov.uk/consultations/downloadableDocs/EveryChildMattersNextSteps.pdf

ECM website www.everychildmatters.gov.uk

The government set out its vision for the improvement in children's services in *Every Child Matters: The next steps* (2004). This suggested that multidisciplinary teams would not only enable information sharing and an early response but also work with the child and family to tailor services to their needs. The considerable challenge in achieving the vision of integrated working is illustrated by the Every Child Matters website listing 14 different professionals or specialists as those who 'might increasingly work together in different types of team.'

Taking forward the aims of Every Child Matters 2004-09

Since the green paper was published in 2003, legislation has been enacted and considerable resources directed to taking forward the Every Child Matters: Change for Children agenda. The Children Act 2004 provides the statutory basis for the establishment of Children's Trusts by setting out a duty for all 'relevant partners' to co-operate in planning and providing services to children and young people in a local authority. The partners are listed as:

> *district councils, the police, the probation board, the youth offending team, the Strategic Health Authority and Primary Care Trusts, Connexions partnerships, and the Learning and Skills Council.*

Other partners, such as schools, have since been added to this list by further legislation.

The Children Act 2004 also established the roles of Directors of Children's Services and Lead Members for Children's Services in each authority and the requirement for every area to produce a Children and Young People's Plan (CYPP). This plan was described as:

> *'...a single, strategic, overarching plan for all services affecting children and young people. This should support more integrated and effective services to secure the outcomes for children set out in Every Child Matters: Change for Children'.*
>
> (Guidance on Children and Young People's Plans 2004)

DIG DEEPER for a list of key documents that explain and shape the strategic direction of the Every Child Matters: Change for Children programme. This provides important context and background to the use of the Tools in the later parts of this Handbook.

The Children Act (2004) www.opsi.gov.uk/acts/acts2004a

Guidance on the Children and Young People's Plan www.everychildmatters.gov.uk/strategy/guidance

Children's Plan: Building brighter futures
www.dcsf.gov.uk/childrensplan/downloads/The_Childrens_Plan.pdf

ECM website www.everychildmatters.gov.uk

The Children's Plan

In 2007 the government published its ten-year national strategy for the further development of children's services – *The Children's Plan: Building brighter futures.* This takes forward the vision and commitments set out in Every Child Matters. Stressing the intention to work in partnership with parents, it sets out the government's plan to:

> *make England the best place in the world for children and young people to grow up.*

The plan also strengthens the role of Children's Trusts as the recognised body providing strategic governance to children and young people's services in every local authority and the vehicle for local delivery of the Every Child Matters agenda.

Workforce development: the 2020 Workforce Strategy

The Children's Workforce Development Council (CWDC) was established in 2005 to support the Every Child Matters agenda. The CWDC

> *is charged with implementing integrated working by closely collaborating with the Department for Children, Schools and Families, local and regional organisations across England, and with the children's private, faith, community and third sector workforce.*
>
> (CWDC website 2009)

The Children's Plan promised a children's workforce action plan to strengthen integrated working across all services and this was launched in the form of the 2020 Children and Young People's Workforce Strategy in December 2008. Steered by an expert group representing the whole of the children and young people's workforce, the strategy recognises that those who work with children and young people are critical to achieving the ambition of making England the best country in the world for children to grow up in.

The 2020 Workforce Strategy describes how 'government will work with partners to ensure that everyone in the workforce receives the support they need'. It identifies 'reforms needed across the whole of the workforce, as well as priorities for the development of each part of it'. A key feature of the strategy is its commitment to:

> *supporting people in the workforce to develop the skills and behaviours they need to work effectively in partnership with children, young people and parents, and with each other, in ways that secure better outcomes.*

The strategy recognises that by working together 'people can make a great difference for children and young people – particularly for those who are most disadvantaged'. However, it acknowledges that there are barriers and challenges to achieving effective integrated working. Addressing those barriers is a priority, and the strategy both outlines existing guidance and tools to support joint working and describes how that support will be developed further.

The strategy also acknowledges that there are current gaps in evidence for the outcomes of integrated working. It sets out the intention to establish a knowledge bank, accessible to the workforce and its managers, that will contain evidence:

> *about the effect that workforce practice and interventions can have on children's outcomes ... including evidence relating to the impact of different approaches to integrated working on outcomes.*

Another new body supporting the move to evidence-informed services for children, the **Centre for Excellence and Outcomes in Children and Young People's Services (C4EO)**, will contribute to the knowledge bank.

Support for integrated practice

Describing what the workforce shares or has in common sets a foundation for integrated practice and helps people to be more aware of similarity than difference. Both the Common Core of Skills and Knowledge and the Children's Workforce Network (CWN) Statement of Values for Integrated working with children and young people, are statements that provide that foundation. The boxes following summarise their content:

Common Core of Skills and Knowledge

The Common Core is made up of six areas of expertise:

- effective communication and engagement
- child and young person development
- safeguarding and promoting the welfare of the child
- supporting transitions
- multiagency working
- sharing information.

The Common Core reflects a set of common values for practitioners that promote equality, respect diversity and challenge stereotypes, helping to improve the life chances of all children and young people and to provide more effective and integrated services. It also acknowledges the rights of children and young people, and the role parents, carers and families play in helping children and young people achieve the outcomes identified in Every Child Matters.

(taken from CWDC website 2009)

DIG DEEPER

Children's Trusts www.everychildmatters.gov.uk/aims/childrenstrusts

Children's Workforce Development Council (strategy)
www.everychildmatters.gov.uk/deliveringservices/childrenandyoungpeoplesworkforce

The Children's Workforce Development Council (CWDC) www.cwdcouncil.org.uk

The 2020 Workforce Strategy 2008
www.everychildmatters.gov.uk/deliveringservices/childrenandyoungpeoplesworkforce

Centre for Excellence and Outcomes (C4EO) www.c4eo.org.uk

The Children's Workforce Network statement of values for integrated working with children and young people

Examples of the statements within it are:

- Children and young people value practitioners who enjoy working with them, who treat them with respect and who are good at communicating with them.
- Practitioners concern themselves with the whole child, whatever their specialism.
- Children's practitioners are committed to equality of opportunity for all children, and actively combat discrimination and its effects through their work. They respond positively and creatively to diversity among children and families, and colleagues.

Reproduced in full as an appendix to Building Brighter Futures: Next steps for the Children's Workforce (Feb 2008)

Alongside the Common Core and the CWN's statement of values for integrated working, both the Every Child Matters and the CWDC websites describe common or shared processes to drive integrated working and provide guidance and training materials to support their implementation. These key processes are described in the box below.

Key integrated processes

1. **Information sharing between professionals**

   Appropriate information sharing underpins all integrated processes. Cross-government guidance has been developed for all practitioners and managers who work with children, young people and families to ensure they understand when, why and how they should share information.

2. **The Common Assessment Framework (CAF) for children and young people**

   The CAF is a key part of delivering front-line services that are integrated and focused around the needs of children and young people.

   The aim is to identify, at the earliest opportunity, a child or young person's additional needs which are not being met by the universal services they are receiving, and provide timely and co-ordinated support to meet those needs.

   The CAF is a standardised approach to conducting an assessment of a child's additional needs and deciding how those needs should be met. It is intended to reduce duplication of assessment, encourage a shared language across agencies and improve referrals between agencies. A national electronic version (eCAF) is planned.

3. **Lead Professionals** Lead Professionals work with children and young people with additional (including complex) needs who require an integrated package of support from more than one practitioner. The Lead Professional is a key element of integrated support. They are described as taking the lead to co-ordinate provision and acting as a single point of contact for a child and their family when a range of services are involved and an integrated response is required. This way all children and young people who require integrated support from more than one practitioner should experience a seamless and effective service.
4. **ContactPoint** ContactPoint is an online directory, available to authorised staff who need it to do their jobs, enabling the delivery of co-ordinated support for children and young people. It is also a vital tool to help safeguard children, helping to ensure that the right agencies are involved at the right time and children do not slip through the net. It is a key element of the Every Child Matters programme to transform children's services by supporting more effective prevention and early intervention. The programme's goal is to improve the health, well-being and safety of all children. At the time of writing (April 2009), ContactPoint is in its first stage of delivery with 17 local authorities.
5. **Team Around the Child** (TAC) is an approach to service provision where a range of agencies work together to help and support an individual child.

(from CWDC website 2009)

Since publication of the Every Child Matters green paper, a menu of guidance and support for the development of integrated working has continued to grow. You can keep in touch with those resources through the websites listed here.

DIG DEEPER to see how we bring together the policy background and research evidence

Common Core of Skills and Knowledge
www.everychildmatters.gov.uk/deliveringservices/commoncore

The Children's Workforce Network
www.childrensworkforce.org.uk

research in practice rapid web-based review 'Prompt': *Multi-professional working: distinct professional identities in multi-professional teams* www.rip.org.uk/prompts (a wealth of related resources) Mapping the Field, evaluated practice, key messages, resources and recent research.

Department for Education and Skills (1998) *Excellence for All Children: Meeting special educational needs.* London. HMSO.
www.teachernet.gov.uk/wholeschool/sen/publications/excellencegp

NHS Health Advisory Service (1995) *Child and Adolescent Mental Health Services: Together we Stand.* London HAS
http://www.hascas.org/hascas_publications_reports.shtml

The death of Baby P: a further report supports the need for integrated practice

From the outset, the Every Child Matters agenda was always acknowledged to be a long-term programme of change that would take ten years before it reached full implementation and effect. Nevertheless, the death of a 17-month-old baby five years into that programme, in a case that had many echoes of the death of Victoria Climbié, caused considerable shock. Baby P died in Haringey in 2007 and his mother and two men living in the house were convicted of killing him or allowing his killing. The family had been known to services throughout much of Baby P's life and many opportunities to intervene to protect him and prevent his death were missed or inadequately followed up.

On 17 November 2008 Ed Balls, Secretary of State for Children, Schools and Families, responded to the death of Baby P by asking Lord Laming 'to provide an urgent report on the progress being made across the country to implement effective arrangements for safeguarding children'.

Lord Laming was asked to:

> *evaluate the good practice that has been developed since the publication of the report of the Independent Statutory Inquiry following the death of Victoria Climbié, to identify the barriers that are now preventing good practice becoming standard practice, and recommend actions to be taken to make systematic improvements in safeguarding children across the country.*

The Protection of Children in England: A progress report was published in March 2009. In it, Lord Laming gives credit to the government for the legislation and guidance put in place over the previous five years, but he also stresses the need to continue the implementation of the changes and calls for 'a step change in the arrangements to protect children from harm'.

Lord Laming's recommendations are for changes to achieve more strategic focus on the task of safeguarding children at every level in the system from government through regions to authority and service level. At national level, he recommends the establishment of:

> *a powerful National Safeguarding Delivery Unit to report directly to Cabinet through the Families, Children and Young People Sub-Committee, and to report annually to Parliament.*

At local authority level, Lord Laming urges that both the council leader and the lead member for children's services should ensure that there is sustained attention to the issue and that Children's Trusts are supported in safeguarding and promoting the welfare of children.

The report calls for more resources to ensure all agencies see safeguarding as their business and to support social workers in the very difficult task they face. It also highlights and stresses the need for adult and children's services to work together to protect children effectively.

There is a necessary focus on safeguarding children and the report has much to say about integrated practice when the prevention of harm is a priority, as well as when work is about prevention and early intervention. Lord Laming begins the chapter titled 'Interagency working' with a quote from a social worker:

> *Relationships are crucial; its not about structures, its about making it work out there for children.*

He goes on to note:

> *co-operative working is increasingly becoming the normal way of working. However good examples of joint working too often rely on the goodwill of individuals.*

Lord Laming notes that real concerns remain about sharing information, particularly among practitioners in health. His recommendation is that every Children's Trust should ensure that all partners are consistently applying the DCSF guidance.

Views on the Common Assessment Framework (CAF) gathered for the report were varied. Some areas reported that the CAF had made a huge positive difference to early identification of children in need, while others said it had caused a lot of confusion. Lord Laming recommends that 'all agencies need further help in using the CAF effectively and in managing the role of the lead professional'.

So as we conclude our consideration of the policy context, and the support available from government agencies for integrated practice, Lord Laming's report following the death of Baby P provides evidence of the limited and variable progress to date – and sets out the challenges that face us as we move forward in achieving the 'step change' that is so clearly needed.

We now move on to look at the theoretical frameworks that underpin research theories.

2
Theoretical frameworks

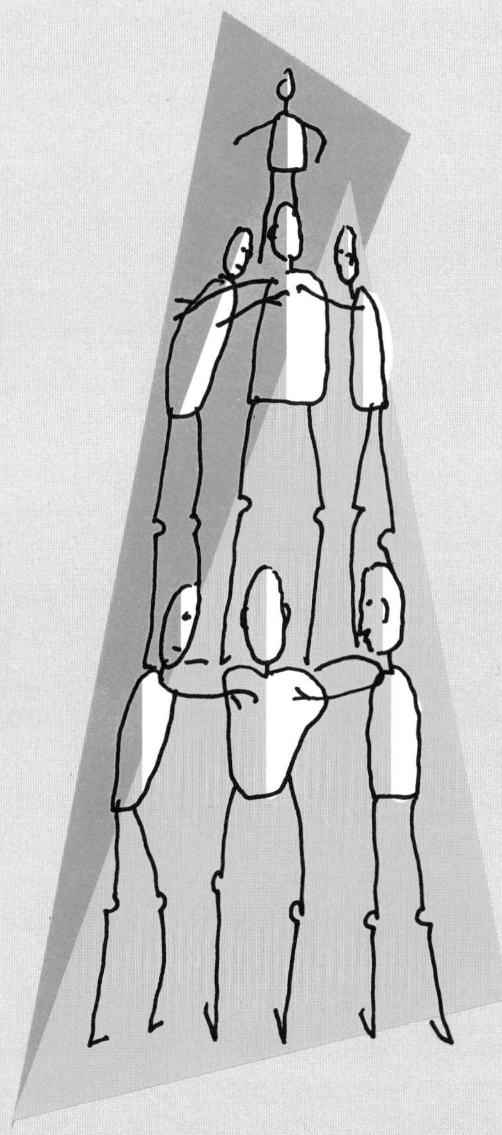

Theoretical frameworks

This chapter introduces and examines some of the key theoretical frameworks underpinning the main sources of research used in this Handbook. This should help your understanding of later sections and help you make best use of the Tools.

The developments that happen in front-line teams or partnerships are not part of formal classroom learning. They happen on the job, so theories of learning and interaction at work are key to understanding how we can support new ways of working that can lead to improved outcomes for children and young people.

Anning et al (2006) draw heavily on the work of two leading theorists: Etienne Wenger and Yrjo Engeström. Wenger's work is in the field of socio-cultural psychology; Engeström's is in knowledge creation and exchange. The work of both is current and very influential in helping us understand how different professionals learn from each other and develop new ways of working as they work more closely together.

Wenger and communities of practice

Wenger (1998) argues that new knowledge is created in what he calls 'communities of practice' by the complementary processes of participation and reification.

- **Participation** can be defined as the daily interactions and shared experiences of members of a community working towards common goals.
- **Reification** is the way that newly generated knowledge is represented in documents or protocols.

> *Wenger points out that professionals construct their identities through their shared practice and joint working. His work can be used to make the point that experienced professionals in multiagency teams will have undergone different historic processes of both self determination and social determination of their professional identity.*
>
> (Anning et al, 2006)

Wenger argues that communities of practice are not necessarily harmonious and co-operative. In essence, his model is about working steadily towards agreement and stability in work-based learning. He measures the extent of joined-up working using these three constructs:

- **mutual engagement** – co-participation, doing things together

- **joint enterprise** – shared accountability, sharing responsibility for joint practice
- **shared repertoire** – shared approaches such as tools, language and actions.

Engeström and activity theory

Engeström's model (2000) draws on activity theory. He stresses that conflict is inevitable as teams work together in new and changing ways. In his view, conflict must be described and explored if progress is to be made in creating new ways of working:

> *In order to effect change, teams and partnerships must work through processes of articulating differences, exploring alternatives, modelling solutions, examining an agreed model and implementing activities.*
>
> (Anning et al, 2006)

'Expansive learning cycles' take place in the workplace when teams come together with different knowledge and expertise to pursue a common goal.

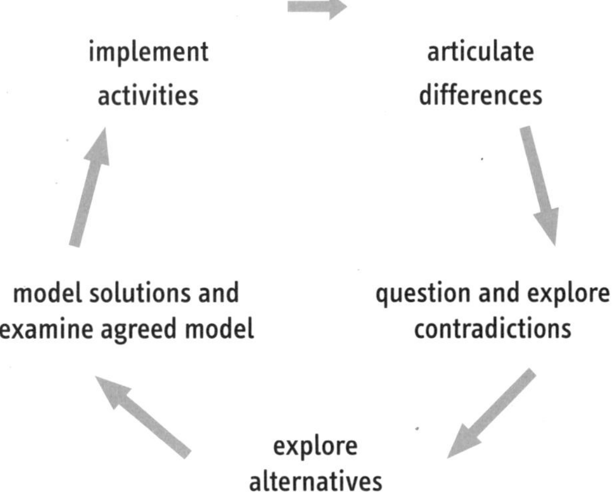

expansive learning cycle (after Engeström, 2000)

DIG DEEPER

Wenger E (1998) *Communities of Practice.* Cambridge: Cambridge University Press

Engeström Y (2000) 'Activity Theory as a Framework for Analyzing and Redesigning Work' Ergonomics 43 (7)

Bowyer S (2008b) **research in practice** rapid web-based review 'Prompt' available at www.rip.org.uk/prompts

Warmington P, Daniels H, Edwards A, Leadbetter J, Martin D, Brown S and Middleton D (2004a) 'Conceptualising Professional Learning for Multi-Agency Working and User Engagement.' British Educational Research Association Annual Conference, UMIST Manchester. Online version available at http://en.scientificcommons.org/8677436

Engeström also argues that change must be linked all the way from the actions at the front line to an articulated and clear vision for the future.

> *A joint enterprise is not about a 'static agreement' between members of a community but is likely to be a process.*
>
> (Anning et al, 2006)

Other researchers (Morrow et al, 2005) have used a psychodynamic model to help to understand the emotions that arise in integrated practice. They note:

> *the success and viability of a social institution are intimately concerned with the techniques it uses to contain anxiety ... An understanding of this aspect of the functioning of a social institution is an important diagnostic and therapeutic tool in facilitating social change [and to] analyze the resistance to and tensions within whole-team meetings.*

What does this mean for effective integrated working?

5

Listen to the group members talking about their experiences of working together in an integrated team, and how they learnt from each other.

Theories of human interaction and learning seem to be particularly relevant to understanding the process of building new ways to work together. They remind us that beliefs, feelings, history and context will all have an impact on the process and that structure and systems can play a role in either holding progress back or supporting effective new ways of working.

Such theories also highlight the potential for resistance and conflict. Effective joined-up working is unlikely to happen without questions or difficulties and, however those difficulties arise, we need to find ways to capture and learn from them. The aim and the potential excitement is that there is 'a radically wider horizon of possibilities than in the previous mode of the activity' (Warmington et al, 2004a).

In the next chapter we will see how these theoretical frameworks have steered researchers to examine the interactions of practitioners involved in integrated practice and to develop tools that aim to improve that practice.

3

What does the research tell us?

What does the research tell us?

This chapter introduces four themes that emerge from the research evidence on integrated working, which are used later in the Handbook to help structure your learning.

The strength of the evidence

The evidence for the effectiveness of integrated working has been reviewed in two important recent studies – Frost (2005) and Anning et al (2006). (Both the Every Child Matters and **research in practice** websites also refer to individual research studies and reviews).

In summarising what the research tells us about integrated working, Frost and Anning et al provide many tips for its successful development (these underpin this Handbook and can be found in the Top Research Tips sections). Their reviews also help by clarifying research implications and identifying where more research is needed.

Evaluation and research on the process of integrated working and learning together is an ongoing task. At this stage all the research used to support this Handbook concludes that the evidence needs to be approached with care and we need to continue to evaluate the work as it becomes more embedded in practice.

Anning et al caution that 'the jury is still out on judgements and effectiveness of reforms'. And while extensive evaluation of programmes such as Sure Start has shown some positive effect for families and children, they also note that 'multiagency working did not appear to be a significant dimension of effectiveness'.

> *It has often proved difficult to establish the exact impact of multiagency working – mainly because of the difficulty of isolating why a particular outcome had been achieved.*
>
> (Every Child Matters website)

Morrow et al (2005) report 'general and anecdotal evidence of impact on individual cases' but concluded it was 'too early to measure overall impact on outcomes.'

A longer-term study by the Local Authority Research Consortium (LARC) to gather evidence of the impact on outcomes is described later in this chapter. In the meantime, despite these cautionary notes, research consistently points to factors that support effective practice – and it is the communication of that information on which this Handbook is firmly based.

Finding out what supports effective practice

Researchers who draw on the theoretical frameworks described above are understandably concerned with the detailed interactions between professionals in integrated practice. Their aim is to find out how best to enable effective joint working so that children and young people can have access to all the skills and knowledge they may need. They also want to find out how new ways of working emerge that can help to overcome difficulty or disadvantage in new ways.

Working with these frameworks, Anning et al (2006) examined the way that people interact in the process of integrated practice, the different language they use and the dilemmas that consistently arise. They found the different professional models that are dominant in training were also evident in practitioners' different approaches to aspects of their work, such as assessments, defining need and describing current problems faced by children and their families.

They also found that asking those working in different multiagency team settings to report 'critical incidents' in their interaction helped expose those aspects of integrated working where dilemmas arose – both for those in the team and those managing them. Their analysis of the discussion of these incidents revealed the different thinking of different professionals and brought to the surface recurring dilemmas that were operating at both team and individual level.

Through a detailed analysis of the conversations that teams had about these incidents, Anning et al found that typical dilemmas emerge. These can be grouped under four themes or headings:

1. **structural issues** – coping with change in systems and management
2. **ideological frameworks** – sharing and redistributing knowledge skills and beliefs
3. **procedural influences** – participation in developing new processes
4. **interprofessional learning** – through role change.

Members of the Change Project groups found these four themes provided some order and structure to help them think about the complex challenge of integrated practice. (They provide the structure for learning about improving your integrated practice in Chapter 5.)

In the following chapters you will find Tools to help you explore the issues that make up these headings. They should help you resolve the sorts of dilemmas and difficulties that can arise in integrated practice.

DIG DEEPER

Frost N (2005) *Professionalism, Partnership and Joined-up Thinking: A research review of front-line working with children and families.* Dartington: **research in practice**
Online version available at www.rip.org.uk/publications/researchreviews.asp

Anning A, Cottrell D, Frost N, Green J and Robinson M (2006) *Developing Multiprofessional Teamwork for Integrated Children's Services.* Maidenhead: Open University Press
Every Child Matters website www.everychildmatters.gov.uk/

The Tools are also linked to a series of practical tips and suggestions – Top Research Tips – that draw on the experience of the Change Project group and on research. Before moving on to those sections, however, we discuss some more recent research, which gives us more learning and examples from practice.

Learning from the range of models of integrated practice as they develop[1]

During the course of this Change Project further research studies have reported, drawing evidence from the models of integrated working that have developed as services to children, young people and their families respond to the Every Child Matters agenda and address the challenge of achieving its aims across the complex pattern of local agencies and services. These reports draw on integrated practice in Children's Centres, extended schools and locality-based systems that bring professionals together. In this section we highlight some of their conclusions and recommendations.

One such study considered the common operational features of effective front-line practice in integrated working and concluded that strong personal relationships were the 'key driving and sustaining force for effective integrated working in all the areas visited'. (DCSF, 2007b) *Effective Integrated Working: Findings of Concept of Operations study*.)

The study also reported that the quality of integration depends greatly on local circumstances. Factors such as resource availability, funding arrangements, historical relationships, workforce stability and the influence of specific managers were all given as explanations for the quality of relationships. The level of engagement of schools was reported to be polarised and dependent on the view of the headteacher.

The researchers conclude that localised integrated working can be seen to provide benefits to children, young people and their families and to practitioners, and that the evidence points to localised integrated working as being a necessary first step towards fully integrated working.

However, they also highlight risks associated with localised integrated working, noting that it is totally dependent on individuals, so that changes in personnel could cause it to falter. Other findings from this study echo those of the two main studies used in this Handbook, adding detail that is highly pertinent to the current context (see box opposite).

Another recent research report provides guidance to school leaders on multiagency working (Coleman, 2006). Schools, of course, have a major role in delivering integrated working through the extended schools programme and the 21st century vision for schools. The report notes that staff from other

[1] This section of the Handbook draws extensively on the **research in practice** online resource 'Prompt 3' *Multi-professional Working: Distinct professional identities in multi-professional teams* (Bowyer, 2008) www.rip.org.uk/prompts/p3/current.asp

Key findings

- **Use of common professional programmes** was one approach that enabled staff to work together more effectively was for the team to adopt specific programmes, such as the Solihull model or the Supporting Families programme for their work with clients.
- **Use of shared facilities** improved opportunities for joint training sessions and meetings.
- **Involvement of children and families** in meetings was found to be a driver for integrated working, helping to drive a holistic view of the child and family's needs by hearing their voices directly.
- **Multiagency training arrangements** are an important vehicle for bringing agencies together to develop skills, raise understanding of the roles of other professionals and build relationships.
- **Involvement of staff** in development of new ways of working was an integral part of developing the service and the team.
- **Implementation of common processes** (such as the CAF and Lead Professional) was seen to have successfully promoted integrated working across a very wide range of services in a relatively short period of time.
- **Building awareness of local services** was essential to be able to identify and involve the most appropriate services to help the child and family.

agencies working in a school setting will need to continue to receive supervision from their own agency to maintain links and ensure professional development, but they will also need supervision from a member of the senior leadership team in the school context. It also notes that change can take a long time, as it is the 'soft' issues of culture and interpersonal relationships that are the most demanding.

The role of social workers

> *In some respects social work's unique position is that it sits at the interface of not only organisational but also conceptual systems. Social work has the capacity to negotiate between different professional perspectives.*
>
> (Blewett et al, 2007, quoted in Moran et al, 2007)

There is currently considerable debate on the future role and task of social workers and, within that, consideration of the use of their skills and knowledge to support models of integrated practice. Evidence and recommendations from two research studies contribute to this discussion:

- Patricia Moran, Catherine Jacobs, Amanda Bunn and Antonia Bifulco (2007) *Multi-agency Working: Implications for an early-intervention social work team* and

- Janice Boddy, Antonia Simon and Valerie Wigfall (2007) *Evaluation of a Link Social Worker Post in Two Islington Children's Centres.*

Both studies examined the role of social workers working alongside other professionals in early intervention services (eg Children's Centre settings) and both concluded that the social workers' contribution to the development of integrated practice was positive. Social workers provided advice and support to other workers, helped their understanding of the role of statutory services and led the implementation of CAF. Both social workers and other practitioners felt that working together had helped them all feel positive about multiagency working. One study reported that social workers felt families were more respectful and less fearful of engaging with a social worker from a multiagency team, while Boddy et al concluded that it was not compatible for a social worker linked to an early intervention team to hold child protection cases. (Bowyer, 2008b)

Research due to report in 2009 and beyond

A further significant research project called *Learning in and for Inter-agency Working* (LIW) took place between 2004 and 2007, and reported early in 2009.

This work also draws on activity theory and the work of Engeström. Like the teams involved in the development of this Handbook, the LIW researchers worked with teams that span most types of practitioner found in children's services and offer 'different configurations of professionals, including new multiprofessional teams and more loosely coupled arrangements of team working' (Edwards et al, 2009). They used a method called Cultural Historical Activity Theory (CHAT) to analyse the conversations across the multiprofessional teams.

The findings echo those of the research reviewed above in many ways. In the research summary, the researchers describe professionals as needing to:

> *understand and talk fluently about their own professional values, about the implications of a multiagency environment for professional values and about their own expertise in order to question and negotiate practice with other professionals.*

DIG DEEPER

Coleman A (2006) *Collaborative Leadership in Extended Schools.* Nottingham: National College for School Leadership Online version available at www.ncsl.org.uk/media-5dd-ec-extended-schools.pdf

Bowyer S (2008b) Prompt 3. *Multi-professional Working: Distinct professional identities in multi-professional teams.* Online **research in practice** resource at www.rip.org.uk/prompts

Moran P, Jacobs C, Bunn A and Bifulco A (2007) *Multi-agency Working: Implications for an early-intervention social work team*

Boddy J, Simon A and Wigfall V (2007) *Evaluation of a Link Social Worker Post in Two Islington Children's Centres.*

They also report that 'interprofessional practices need encouraging organisational climates that allow for professional decision making rather than rigid co-ordination'.

Another key research initiative is being led by the Local Authority Research Consortium (LARC) project. LARC was formed at the start of 2007 and is made up of four organisations: the National Foundation for Educational Research, the Improvement and Development Agency, **research in practice** and the Local Government Association. Working with volunteer local authorities, its aim is to monitor progress on integrated working and whether that impacts on the five Every Child Matters outcomes for children and their families.

In its round one reporting (2007-08) based on work in 14 local authorities, LARC found that successful authorities were characterised by clarity of purpose, strong leadership and management, the development of a common language, trust between partners and understanding responsibilities (Lord et al, 2008, cited by Bowyer, 2008a).

The LARC findings are grouped into four levels of impact:

- level 1 changes to inputs and structures
- level 2 changes to experience and attitudes
- level 3 changes to outcomes for children and young people in specific groups
- level 4 institutional or systemic embedding of change.

Despite the recognised difficulty of measuring a direct impact on outcomes for children from integrated working, the LARC (round one) report identifies impacts for looked after children, those in the autistic spectrum group and those at Key Stage 3. It shows clear variation between 'confidently integrated authorities' and others, identifying impacts at levels 1 to 3, such as reductions in referrals to acute services, improved stability of placements, improved attendance and an improved range of services to support children and their families.

LARC (Round 2), involving 33 authorities, is now underway (2009) and will consider how far the CAF process supports the achievement of better outcomes for children and young people, also looking at the key factors that promote the effectiveness of CAF in different contexts.

DIG DEEPER

Edwards A, Daniels H, Gallagher T, Leadbetter J and Warmington P (2009) *Improving Inter-professional Collaborations: Multi-agency working for children's well-being.* London and New York: Routledge

Warmington P, Daniels H, Edwards A, Leadbetter J, Martin D, Brown S and Middleton D (2004b) Learning in and for interagency working: conceptual tensions in 'joined up' practice. *TLRP Annual Conference.* Cardiff.

Lord et al (Local Authorities Research Consortium) (2008) *Evaluating the Early Impact of Integrated Children's Services.* Online version available at www.nfer.ac.uk/research-areas/pims-data/summaries/larc.cfm

4

Getting started – describing the way that integrated practice is being delivered where you are

Getting Started

This chapter sets out four steps to help you get started.

By following these steps, you will be able to:

- *identify all those factors that drive or impede integrated working on the front line*
- *describe the nature of the practice where you are*
- *say clearly which stage of development you are in, ie where you are now and where you aim to be.*

Opportunities and threats
Use Tool 1 to identify those factors that, from a practitioner's point of view, will help drive integrated practice – and those factors that will restrain its progress.

Step One: Identifying sources of support and potential barriers

You can start by using Tool 1 to help you find sources of support for the process of working together – and to identify those things that might get in the way.

Step Two: Describing the structure and governance of integrated practice where you are

There are considerable variations in models of delivering integrated practice, the ways in which workers relate to join up their work, and the needs they seek to address. It is important that you can identify where your practice is placed in relation to those dimensions: the range of practitioners; who employs them; how they are managed; how work is co-ordinated; and whether practitioners work full time or not. The list of dimensions is referred to in Tool 2.

Understanding your team
Use Tool 2 to help you describe and understand how integrated practice is delivered where you are working. You can do this either as a group or as individuals.

> *The way services from a range of professions are arranged may seem to promise joined-up working, but it is the way the teams are organised and managed (from both within and without the team) that dictates how effectively they are able to work together.*
>
> Anning et al, 2006

Spending some time making sure you have a clear understanding of the model that is operating where you work, and the stage of development you are in (see step 4), can help you in a number of ways.

- It should enable you to make comparisons, use evidence effectively and learn from others.
- It will be a useful source of material for induction – in other words, for telling others about how you work.
- You can use what you learn as the basis for creating leaflets or web material about your service.

You can see what members of the Change Project groups said about learning from each other by watching the third film on the videoCD.

The table shows how some of the teams in the Change Project groups explained and categorised themselves using Tool 2.

Teams and services in the first Change Project group

Type of team	Structure to deliver integrated practice	Governance or partnership arrangements
Multidimensional Treatment Foster Care	Integrated team. Staff from a range of backgrounds recruited or seconded specifically to the tea	Management group of partner agencies
A project safeguarding children and young people who are victims of sexual exploitation	Mixture of permanent and seconded staff	Joint senior management group
Specialist children's service – for disabled children and their families	Partnership involving health (PCT), social care and education – 100 staff in all	Joint senior management group

Step Three: Using maps to describe integrated practice

Tool 2 includes some examples of the diagrams or maps (Anning et al, 2006). These show how a diagram can help you understand integrated working – and explain it to others.

Understanding models of integrated practice through spatial maps

You can also use Tool 2 to produce diagrams or spatial maps that illustrate how integrated practice works where you are. These should set out how work is co-ordinated and how workers are supervised and managed. They can be useful for induction for new staff and for explaining to service users who is who and how the service works.

The fully managed team

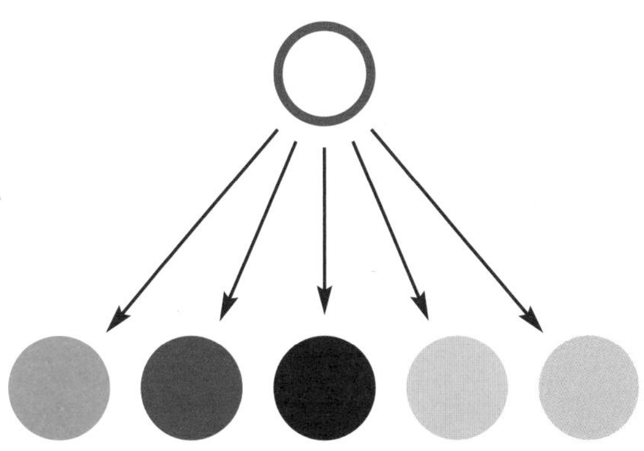

The core and extended team

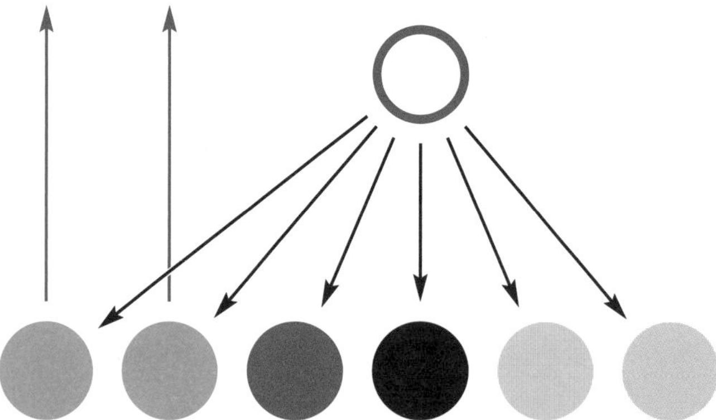

You can also produce diagrams to show more explicitly which agencies are involved in the team and how. Here are two more diagrams from Anning et al (2006); you will find the full set of diagrams reproduced as part of Tool 2.

Step Four: Considering the model of integration that will be effective where you are

TOOL 3

How joined-up are you?
Use Tool 3 to describe the model of integrated practice where you are. You may find that some services work alongside you under the same manager while others stand outside that arrangement. You can do this exercise as a group or as individuals. Interestingly, when the Change Project groups tried this, different members of the same team placed themselves in different places along the continuum. Such differences can form the basis for discussion.

Frost (2005) describes joined–up working as a progression through different levels. (We should be clear that no single model is seen as a better way to deliver integrated practice than others.)

1. **Level one: co-operation.** Services work together towards consistent goals and complementary services, while maintaining their independence.
2. **Level two: collaboration.** Services plan together and address issues of overlap, duplication and gaps in service provision towards common outcomes.
3. **Level three: co-ordination.** Services work together in a planned and systematic manner towards shared and agreed goals.
4. **Level four: merger/'full' integration.** Different services become one organisation in order to enhance service delivery.

Here's an example from the Change Project teams. This table shows how they indicated their current levels of integration, and where they aim to be.

	1 co-operation	2 collaboration	3 co-ordination	4 merger/ integration	
Treatment foster care service (management group)	NOW	AIM			Scored **level 1** now and aiming for **level 2.** This indicates that the management group is currently un-coordinated and knows that it would improve integrated practice if it developed that co-ordination.
Treatment foster care service (practitioners)		NOW	AIM		Scored **level 2** now and aiming for **level 3.** The team want to be more joined-up, moving on from day-to-day joint working to planning together.
Service set up to improve CAF through information sharing	NOW		AIM		Scored level 1 now and aiming for **level 3.** This team felt they were currently un-coordinated and they needed to be working together more closely and jointly planning.
Specialist service for disabled children and their families			NOW	AIM	Scored **level 3** now and aiming for **level 4.** This team already work in a co-ordinated way and they felt the service would work more effectively if it were fully integrated.

Of course, the model of working that a group of staff aspire to may not be possible to achieve without support from senior managers. These exercises will help a group of staff to talk through how they work now and to identify change that could support improved practice.

Action plan
You are most likely to make progress with integrated working if you break down the tasks you have to do into small steps and then identify the actions you need to take for each step. Many action plans fail because the tasks appear too difficult. You may have several goals but you need to break each down into a list of tasks. Set a timescale for each action, but be realistic – do not expect the impossible.

If you have used all the suggested Tools in this section, then you should now be able to:

- describe integrated practice where you are
- be clear how it is managed
- be clear which stage of development it is in
- and be clear how it relates to the agencies involved.

You will also have considered some ways in which the team might take action to improve its working. You may want to gather those actions to start building an action plan using Tool 14.

5
Improving integrated practice – a detailed assessment of your progress

Improving integrated practice

This chapter uses the four themes that emerge from the research evidence and which were described in Chapter 3.

1. *Structural issues - systems and management*
2. *ideological frameworks - sharing skills and beliefs*
3. *procedural influences - developing new processes*
4. *interprofessional learning - through role change.*

It includes questionnaires to help you audit your practice and decide where to focus your efforts. It also provides tools, guidance and tips to help you develop plans for achieving more effective integrated working.

Because it promises the prospect of new ways of working, integrated practice can feel exciting. There are things that can get in the way, however. In Chapter 4 ('Getting started'), we suggested you use Tool 1 ('Opportunities and threats') to identify the factors that can impede progress. The flip chart below shows some of the barriers identified by one of the Change Project workshops. As you work your way through the four themes in this chapter, bear in mind both the barriers and the factors that help.

Barriers to integrated practice

- Lack of support from wider structures and organisations can make a team feel vulnerable and undervalued.
- Multiagency working needs wider systemic support.
- There will be challenges to established systems and expectations.
- Difficulties in getting the space and equipment to support effective co-location or even joint activities can make interaction difficult to achieve.
- People who don't want to engage pose a risk to the whole of the intent.
- Communication is a major issue – if it fails, some people feel left out, or myth and rumour can take over.
- There are mixed messages at play – powerful messages about integration, but budget problems in one or more agencies mean it's difficult to get on with the job.
- Different terms and conditions of employment can get in the way of joint working.

As you work through this chapter, use Tools 4 to 7 to help you audit your work across each of the four themes. These will help you decide where to focus your efforts.

1 Structural issues – systems and management

Integrated working in front-line teams requires:

- clear objectives
- effective and confident governance and management.

The advantages of working together can be lost if staff have to refer back to separate systems for permission and agreement about everyday working. The benefits can also be lost if it isn't clear how work will be co-ordinated or if those who work part time don't feel included.

Research has shown that co-location can help (Frost, 2005). But if staff have not been consulted on the move and lose personal space, or if there are still no systems to support more interaction, then a physical change of location may have little effect at best – and a negative impact at worst. The assumed effect of being in the same building is that people will interact and get to know each other; this does not necessarily happen, however. One team involved in the Change Project were based in the same building, but it was only after discussion at an away day that a decision was taken to leave open the doors between the rooms in which different professional groups were based and to form a joint tea club. Whether based in one building or not, it is clear efforts have to be made to spend time together and get to know and trust each other.

It's also important that the organisations staff have come from (sometimes referred to as the 'stakeholding agencies') are supportive of integrated working. Have they been sold the idea as an important opportunity? Have managers considered how they will remain in touch with seconded staff and support their work? Are the ways of reporting back established so that problems can be resolved? Will successes be celebrated?

Checklist: Structural issues - systems and management
Use it to help you work out how well the integrated practice where you are is supported by systems and structures. Remember, you can use this Tool individually and then come together as a team to discuss any differences. The Tool should also help you identify and address any gaps or problems.

In some instances, developments to support integrated working rely on short-term funding. Practitioners and managers who move into posts to support such developments are offered only temporary posts. Working in such teams is valuable experience, but if their establishment is not supported by long-term plans or secure funding it can mean an unpredictable future and so feel risky.

The agencies involved need to think through their joint decision making and planning processes, and establish clear and transparent arrangements. Different terms and conditions of employment can cause tensions when people try to work together. Realistically, some of these differences cannot be addressed locally; they are enshrined in the different histories of parts of the workforce. However, acknowledging and understanding that those differences exist – and making some joint decisions about how you will work together – can avoid feelings of exploitation or dissatisfaction.

The government's very clear support for the development of integrated working (through the Children's and Young People's Plan and the tools and guidance provided by both the Every Child Matters and the Children's Workforce Development Council websites) now provides a secure and supportive context for integrated practice in children and young people's services. Where the Children's Trust arrangements in a local authority are well developed, teams will be part of a local Children and Young People's Plan– so they will know where they sit in the wider picture and should be supported at every level in working together to improve outcomes for children.

However, many authorities are still on the journey towards robust Children's Trust arrangements and it remains essential to use messages from research to help to realise the benefits of integrated working.

Here are some research tips to help strengthen structures, systems and management.

1. Effective integrated practice needs to be supported by clear objectives that have been agreed by all the agencies involved.
2. There need to be clear workload or performance targets that have been agreed by all the agencies involved. (These should be set out in the Children and Young People's Plan for the area.)
3. Effective integrated teams need to have authority to make decisions about their day-to-day working (as long as these are in accord with agreed targets and objectives).
4. Whatever the structure or model of integrated practice, there must be clarity about line-management arrangements.
5. Clear mechanisms must exist for co-ordinating work.
6. It can help if team members are co-located, but regular and effective interaction can be supported in other ways.
7. Effective integrated practice needs structures for communicating with all the agencies involved.
8. There also need to be clear mechanisms in place for informing and involving part-time workers about what has taken place in their absence.
9. Integrated practice cannot ignore inequalities caused by different terms and conditions across the professions involved.

4

Watch the fourth film on the videoCD to see what participants in the Change Project groups had to say about the effect of integrated practice on outcomes for service users.

1

See what participants in the Change Project groups had to say about the effect of co-location on integrated working. Watch the first film on the videoCD.

'If the organisation goes belly up, workers on permanent contracts have confidence they'll be re-employed. Those on short-term contracts don't have this confidence.'

'Outcomes must shift the mindset. Isn't that what they are for?'

'Workers should make it their own target to focus on the child.'

And here are some practical things you can do...

...to reinforce clear objectives

'Retell the story of the 'journey' to better working together.'

'Provide staff with a structure chart to explain accountability.'

...to strengthen structures for communicating with partner agencies

'Have the names and photographs of senior managers on the staff noticeboard.'

...to minimise inequalities

'Make staff job titles more equitable.'

'Create systems for single access to learning and development opportunities related to the joint working.'

'Liaise with Human Resources re salary levels and terms and conditions.'

'Be clear about differing service conditions from the outset and do whatever is possible to even these out.'

'Make use of joint training.'

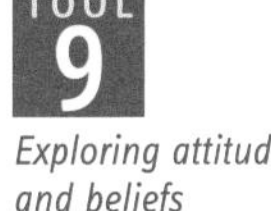

Exploring attitudes and beliefs
Use Tool 9 to understand and reflect on your experience of integrated working.

Clear systems for communicating

In an integrated service to disabled children and young people, a weekly fun and movement group was summarily cancelled when one member of staff phoned in sick. There were four different disciplines involved in running the group and none was consulted on the decision to cancel. Following this incident, all the staff involved met. They agreed that in the event of any one of them being sick, the other staff involved would be informed – and that the group would go ahead as long as at least two of the four were working.

2 Ideological frameworks – sharing and redistributing knowledge, skills and belief

Professionals who have been trained through the same academic path generally work together without explaining why they work in the way that they do. The reasons for this lie in the commonality of the theoretical models, values and beliefs they use to assess a child or family's needs, or to decide what intervention to use. Only in training situations or during induction are these underlying factors made explicit.

Differences in those models, values and beliefs can emerge as conflicts in integrated teams, however. There are likely to be significant differences in how practitioners from different professional backgrounds respond to a presented need or situation – for example, a health visitor and early years worker are likely to have different approaches to standards of care for a young child, and a foster carer and social worker may disagree about a young person's leisure activities. Recent research on Youth Offending Teams notes such differences between police and other agencies:

> *A police culture of rapid reaction or 'action orientation' contrasted with other agencies' preference for consultation and reflection before making major decisions.*
>
> (Ellis and Boden, 2005)

Sometimes there are also perceived hierarchies of status across the professions that work with children and families. As a result, some practitioners may expect their own views to overrule those of others or assume that they will lead team decision making. Other practitioners may have experience of their own views being discounted.

Some conflict in integrated practice is a strong possibility. Indeed, as we saw earlier, Engeström sees conflict as an essential pre-requisite for learning and for new ways of working to emerge. Nevertheless, that process has to be managed and used constructively. If people don't feel heard, they may be overpowered by feelings of disorientation and so disengage from the new ways of working.

> *Different professional voices have a right to be heard within multiprofessional teamwork. For many professionals who have been catapulted into multiprofessional teamwork the emotional aspects of coping with change in their working lives are underestimated both in the preparation and training offered to members of multiprofessional teams.*
>
> (Anning et al, 2006)

Models of supervision in integrated practice are developing and being disseminated by the Children's Workforce Development Council. It is important

Opportunities and threats
Use Tool 1 to identify the factors that will help you move to integrated practice and those that will get in the way.

Common Core of Skills and Knowledge

that workers have supervision from someone who knows about their professional practice and that there is appropriate supervision of the integrated working. In most situations, this can be achieved by making specialist supervision available where professionals have a manager from a different discipline. This also ensures continuing professional development and a link to peers.

Discussing the Common Core or the Children's Workforce Network statement of values for integrated working can provide a useful and positive background for reflecting on different approaches or values. Both demonstrate that there is commonality across the workforce and that everyone in it shares the aim of improving outcomes for children and young people. Exploring and understanding differences in this wider context can be less threatening and instead become a learning opportunity.

Top Research Tips

Here are some practical things you can do...

1. Different theoretical models must be respected when you work with other professions.
2. Different professional groups must be accorded equal respect.
3. Supervision should be attuned to the needs of individuals within the team and their various professional backgrounds.
4. Practitioners need to be encouraged to share skills and ideas with each other.
5. There needs to be an awareness of the impact of integrated working on the professional identity of workers – and on service users.

TOOL 5

Checklist: Idealogical frameworks - sharing and redistributing knowledge, skills and beliefs
Use Tool 5 as an audit to help you decide where you need to focus your efforts on making improvements – and achieving more effective integrated working.

The flip chart below shows some of the concerns about integrated working that were raised in one of the Change Project workshops.

We're concerned...
- about loss of professional identity
- about loss of professional status
- about different hierarchical structures in other partner agencies, eg, health
- about loss of professional skill base when specialist teams become centralised.

Here are some practical things you can do...

...to ensure different theoretical models are respected

'Be aware that jargon can exclude some practitioners. Don't use it!'

'Make it explicit that if anyone doesn't know what something means, they just ask.'

'Be explicit about different underlying models.'

...to ensure different theoretical models are respected

'Don't jump to be directive – explore why it's happening and see it as an opportunity to learn.'

3 Procedural influences – participation in developing new processes

Dedicated time is needed to develop new ways of working and then to capture them in new procedures and protocols. You need to work out together what is needed – and then review and adjust the way you work in the light of feedback.

Morrow et al (2005) describe the confusion that arose in a Sure Start referral and action working group when there were no established procedures. The group were able to progress integrated practice by establishing whole-staff meetings with agreed purpose and shared objectives to manage the referrals. After a year there was evidence that the system was working effectively, although there was still some tension and resistance in team meetings.

The context in which integrated working is operating is still developing. That context will also differ from one agency to another. The key processes of the Common Assessment Framework, Lead Professional and information sharing are important tools to support integrated working. These should be in use across all authorities under the auspices of the Children and Young People's Trust. Existing teams and services that have developed their own systems will need to work out how those interact with local trust-wide systems. Where there are new structures to support integrated practice, practitioners will be able to use them to provide a head start in terms of common systems and processes.

Even where services or localities are employing nationally designed systems or where they can use procedures created elsewhere, they will still need to adapt them to their local system and introduce them through joint training.

A practical problem, for example, is the ambitious national agenda around the storage of information and the use of IT systems to support improved practice and performance management. It will not always be possible across a locality or Children's Trust to use one system for case records (different agencies may be using different IT systems) and there will often be uncertainty about the sharing of information and concerns about confidentiality. The DCSF guidance on information sharing assists with this; a training session for the team using this guidance should help you draft a protocol that provides clarity and is acceptable to all agencies involved.

Speed Dating
This 'speed dating' exercise may help to dispel some of the differences that might be encountered and will certainly help you to get to know more about each other's approach.

Undertaking joint visits or assessments can also be fraught with misunderstanding if roles and responsibilities are not agreed. Describing to service users what other parts of the team or partnership will or can do requires a good understanding of other professional skills and modes of working, so there is no substitute for time spent getting to know each other's roles and agreeing how you will work together.

TOOL 6

Checklist: Procedural influences - participation in developing new processes
Explore how well your team is doing in developing appropriate processes and procedures to support integrated practice. Use this audit to help you decide where to focus your efforts to make further improvements.

The following activities have all been shown to help in overcoming the sorts of dilemmas and difficulties described above.

1. New processes to meet shared objectives need to be designed for and adopted by all those seeking to develop integrated practice, whether in a team or across a locality.
2. Procedures that pre-date integrated practice within an agency or service need to be reviewed to ensure they do not impede the objective of working together.
3. Undertaking joint client-focused activities (such as shared assessment and/or consultation with families) with colleagues with whom you wish to develop integrated practice will help you work together effectively.
4. There should be regular opportunities for discussion of those joint client-focused activities.
5. All agencies involved should continue to provide ongoing support for the professional development of their staff involved in integrated working, as well as supporting opportunities for multiagency development.

Here are some practical things you can do...

...to provide opportunities for reflection on practice

'Make space to discuss how things could be done differently. Hold bi-monthly reflective meetings.'

'Video-monitor team meetings in order to look at process.'

'Establish team meetings and away days.'

'Protect an hour of meetings for development work.'

'Hold steering-group meetings with senior managers and stakeholders.'

'Set up means of debriefing on individual cases.'

'Use supervision productively.'

'Schedule team-planning days into people's diaries.'

'Slow down the change process – check what "change process" means for everyone involved .'

'Acknowledge that integrated working takes time.'

'Take account of part-time workers and crisis workers and their needs and involvement.'

'Find a learning mentor or champion.'

...to ensure you have effective processes and procedures

'Build in regular reviews, evaluations and audits as the scope and pace of integrated working grows and changes.'

'Constantly review all documents, forms and templates, processes and admin systems.'

'Review cascade systems for communicating information as these can get stretched as you work with more agencies.'

...to get all agencies involved to continue to support development opportunities

'Make this issue part of the report to the Children's Trust or other interagency body.'

...to find ways of resolving problems together

'Focus on outcomes – this should get the group to work towards solutions.'

'Share your experiences of successful policy change so that the group can analyse and learn from the process.'

'Focus on evidence – and focus on shared vision, values and objectives.'

'Use vignettes to help with this issue.'

'Make contact with similar teams or networking organisations like **research in practice.***'*

...to promote information sharing

'Create an information sharing protocol and get it agreed with all agencies.'

'Set up training on information sharing so staff can rehearse situations they may be concerned about.'

'Have a flow chart showing the process on the team walls or website.'

eg

Establishing clear lines of accountability

In a service to promote improved information sharing, co-ordinate the use of the Common Assessment Framework and the identification of Lead Professionals. The use of the questionnaire about structural systems (Tool 4) revealed that management staff felt 'lost', 'un-supported', 'cross and upset' because there wasn't a senior manager from any of the agencies involved carrying direct responsibility for the service.

In response, front-line managers (in consultation with the staff group) compiled agreed joint protocols and presented these to the senior managers' group for ratification. As a result, workers are now able to seek out support from the appropriate manager and to shape the service further through the establishment of clear routes for influence and operational management.

Information sharing

DIG DEEPER for the government's practitioners' guide to information sharing.
Go to www.everychildmatters.gov.uk/resources-and-practice/IG00065

TOOL 2

Exploring boundaries
You can use Tool 2 to produce diagrams showing which agencies are involved in the team and how.

TOOL 6

Checklist: Procedural influences - participation in developing new processes
Explore how well your team is doing in developing appropriate processes and procedures to support integrated practice. Use this audit to help you decide where to focus your efforts to make further improvements.

TOOL 12

Using common language
Using the Tool about common language can help you make progress on some of these issues. Use this Tool to explain those core terms and definitions that can be interpreted differently by practitioners working in a multiagency setting and so lead to misunderstandings between different professions.

If integrated working is to deliver improved outcomes for children then the practitioners need to find ways to work together.

> *By working together professionals develop a better understanding of diverse and different models.*
>
> *By merging models (quite literally creating joined-up thinking) professionals can share a common model of understanding and this can act as basis for practice.*
>
> *Professionals in joined-up teams find that their identity changes as they become part of a community of practice.*
>
> (Frost, 2005)

Earlier in this chapter (under discussion of the second theme 'ideological frameworks'), we referred to the different professional models that are dominant in training. We pointed out how those models are often evident in the different approaches practitioners take to assessment, defining need and the problems children and their families face.

As a result of these underlying differences, many practitioners see and feel a difference in how they think about themselves as they become involved in integrated working. This is not necessarily positive. We need to acknowledge that change is not always comfortable or easy. But certain factors will provide a secure and safe context to help staff feel able to listen to and learn from each other and to consider new ways of working together.

Effective leadership will be a critical factor in creating that positive context for the emergence of new ways of working. It is also important that roles are clear, that every team member feels valued and that no individuals are allowed to dominate.

> *We would argue that managing multiprofessional teams requires an approach to leadership that maintains a sense of overall direction while being ready to adapt to changes in team membership and workplace priorities. To be a good manager you have to be a chameleon, responding appropriately to changing circumstances.*
>
> (Anning et al, 2006)

Research has shown that effective leaders of integrated practice can span boundaries (Frost, 2005). Consider this quote from Anning et al (2006) in which the authors cite the work of Skelcher and colleagues:

> *We identified a number of boundary-spanning individuals who operated as entrepreneurs in creating new solutions to public policy problems. They had well-developed skills at mobilising political, financial and technical*

TOOL 2

Understanding your team
Explore how your team links to other organisations or agencies – and then consider how to improve those links and overcome any of the negative effects of boundaries. There are three sections to this Tool, which should help you understand how integrated practice is delivered where you are working.

resources from a range of sources and bringing these to bear on particular needs and issues – they start from the problem rather than the procedures.

Boundaries are important because their existence can lead to misunderstandings, lack of communication, duplication or competition. So spanning or breaking down boundaries is an important way to generate new ways of working.

White and Featherstone (2005) suggest that people involved in integrated practice might judge how well they are working together by seeking evidence of their ability to:

- *challenge over-adherence to professional boundaries*
- *establish a shared language for the team, partners, children and young people and carers who use the service*
- *and alter language specific to sub-groups of the full team, which can make those outside that group feel excluded or lead to misunderstanding.*

So how can we create the right context for practitioners involved in integrated working to use their collective knowledge base to work in new and more effective ways? And how will we know if they are doing this successfully?

Top Research Tips

Here are some tips...

1. Integrated practice needs committed and clear leadership.
2. Different roles should be clearly described and understood.
3. When practitioners come together to support a child no one should dominate.
4. The contribution of part-time or peripheral workers must be recognised.
5. Practitioners should be supported in retaining their specialist skills.
6. Practitioners should be able to learn new ways to practice from each other.

2

Listen to what the Change Project groups had to say about effective leadership for integrated working. Watch the second film on the videoCD.

3

And listen to what members of the Change Project groups had to say about learning from each other in integrated working. Watch the third film on the videoCD.

'Differences are OK between us because it means we pick up on different things.'

'We see people with new skill sets emerging. An example is practitioners helping in the design of the Integrated Children's System (ICS) [the systems that hold an electronic record]. They are professional children's workers who also have considerable knowledge and understanding of ICT and how it can help deliver improved services.'

TOOL
7

Checklist: Interprofessional learning - through role change
Carry out an audit to help you evaluate progress on interprofessional learning in your integrated practice. This will help you decide where to focus your efforts.

And here are some practical things you can do...

...to engage part-time workers

'Keep them updated on integrated practice.'

'Ask their opinions on progress and make sure there is space for them to contribute their learning and experience.'

...to clarify roles and responsibilities

'Share job descriptions and update them to reflect new ways of working.'

'Make explicit how each profession will engage with integrated working.'

...to learn from each other

'Hold training sessions or reflection meetings.'

'Hold clinical meetings or carers' meetings.'

'Maintain regular supervision.'

'Carry out joint visits, joint enquiries and joint investigations.'

'Allow time for different agencies to speak about their work, or a particular aspect of it, which others might benefit from.'

'Ask practitioners to share examples of something they have recently learned from working with a partner from another agency.'

'Collect examples of successful joint working and hold a record of them.'

'Set up monthly team presentations on a specific role, what they do, etc. Hold getting-to-know-you events (speed dating!).'

'Hold team briefings at which you find out about each other's roles.'

eg

Engaging peripheral team members

A health worker was appointed some time after a multiagency team was first established. Her job description was not very detailed but others assumed she would develop the role after her appointment. It was assumed there would be plenty of interaction around the managers.

In reality, the appointed person revealed that she felt everyone knew what they were doing – except her! She felt her midwifery background was not being used and that she was expected to operate in a social work role.

The manager concluded that they needed a formal way of giving people opportunities to interact early on with others in the team. The team realised that induction is very important – and that it is difficult to join a team late.

The health worker reported that while she was unclear about her role, her confidence had dipped and she felt 'completely out of her comfort zone'. She also felt that the building (a police station) was a hostile environment and she didn't know how she would get clinical supervision. This issue was identified by the team using one of the Tools in this Handbook, which they felt helped them to name and then address this problem.

In consultation with the health worker, the team took action to make better use of her skills and overcome the uncomfortable feelings. Taking into account what the worker was comfortable with, clinical supervision was arranged, the role was narrowed down, opportunities for using her health knowledge and skills were identified and joint working was more clearly defined and described.

DIG DEEPER

- *Championing Children: A shared set of skills, knowledge and behaviours for those leading and managing integrated children's services* at www.everychildmatters.gov.uk/_files/Championing%20Children%20Single%20Pg.pdf
- Common Core of Skills and Knowledge at www.everychildmatters.gov.uk/deliveringservices/commoncore
- Children's Workforce Development Council work at www.cwdcouncil.org.uk
- Sector Qualifications Strategies at www.cwdcouncil.org.uk/projects/sectorqualificationsstrategy.htm
- Integrated Qualifications Framework at www.iqf.org.uk
- **research in practice**'s Handbook, Leading Evidence-Informed Practice at www.rip.org.uk/publications/handbooks.asp
- The Early Support training programme developed and delivered by a multiagency group of staff to a multiagency audience, including parents and carers: www.earlysupport.org.uk/training
- The National College for School Leadership's guidance on collaborative leadership in extended schools at www.ncsl.org.uk/media/56A/55/collaborative-leadership-in-extended-schools.pdf

6

Paying attention to involving service users, governance, evaluation and action planning

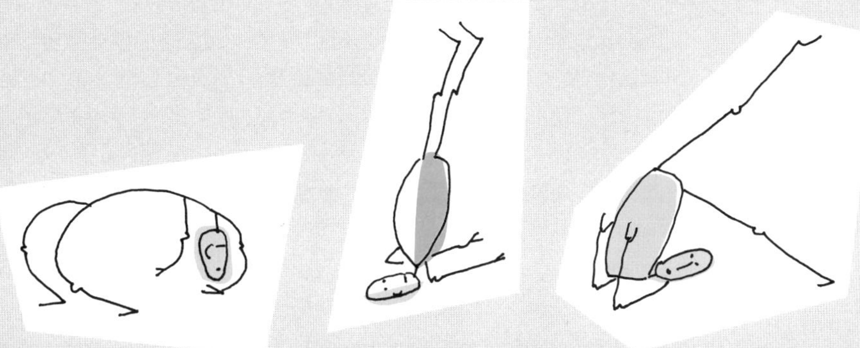

Paying attention to involving service users, governance, evaluation and action planning

This chapter will help you think about some additional issues that are important to effective integrated practice:

- *working with service users*
- *governance arrangements*
- *measuring progress by embedding evaluation in your plans to improve integrated practice on the front line.*

TOOL 10

Common Core of Skills and Knowledge
See how you score out of the 36 requirements for the Common Core of Skills and Knowledge for the Children's Workforce.

Effectively involving parents, carers, children and young people

Effective communication and engagement with children, young people their families and carers is listed as part of the Common Core of Skills and Knowledge for the Children's Workforce. An explicit message in Every Child Matters, the Children's Plan and the workforce strategy is that new ways of working should actively involve service users as partners. The skills and knowledge to support that involvement are therefore central to effective integrated working.

In their review of messages from research for costs and outcomes in children's services, Beecham and Sinclair (2007) conclude that when it comes to user involvement, 'services have not moved on much, if at all, in the direction implied by earlier critiques'. And the direction implied was that services should adopt approaches that were 'based on partnership and prevention'. In other words, services should intervene earlier and address a child's problems in the round, being concerned to support as well as protect.

DIG DEEPER

Jennifer Beecham and Ian Sinclair's review of messages from research, *Cost and Outcomes in Children's Social Care: Messages from research*, published in 2007. Go to www.everychildmatters.gov.uk/resources-and-practice/RS00026

Every Child Matters Common Core of skills and Knowledge www.everychildmatters.gov.uk/deliveringservices/commoncore/

Hear by Right toolkit http://hbr.nya.org.uk/pages/about_hear_right

SCIE's Practice Guide 11 (2005): *Involving Children and Young People in Developing Social Care.* This includes a section (containing a resource tool box and case studies) on involving children and young people in meetings, forums and boards. www.scie.org.uk/publications/guides/guide11/index.asp

r u OK? Website www.ru-ok.org.uk

Parent Participation: Improving services for disabled children. A guide for professionals produced by Contact a Family and the Council for Disabled Children www.cafamily.org.uk/ContactProf05.pdf This guide covers the key principles involved in successful participation. It is practical in approach, and details methods and good practice. The guide is illustrated by many real-life examples.

Meeting with respect pack, Barnardo's. www.barnardos.org.uk/resources/research_and_publications/books_and_tools_participation_and_citizenship.htm A resource pack for professionals who want to develop child-centred meetings in any area of social work. It includes ideas and games to engage children, from before the meeting begins to debriefing together afterwards. Sample child-friendly forms are included.

TOOL 8

Focus on outcomes
Use Tool 8 to help you set out clear objectives for integrated working. Focusing on outcomes is one of the ways in which people can work together across disciplines and with families.

It is important that workers see families as having strengths, alongside their presenting difficulties, and that they are able to work with mothers, fathers and carers to enable them to develop skills and maintain or resume care of their children. Workers, then, should become 'allies of families'; in order to achieve this, they need 'to have the characteristics of accessibility, reliability, practicality that ... families value'. (Beecham and Sinclair, 2007)

The flip chart below shows some of the questions and suggestions raised in one of the Change Project workshops.

Barriers and challenges identified by workers

- How do we get wide enough representation of service users?
- How do we help service users to say what they really feel?
- Views and feedback ARE important but we should be more skilled at getting those views and using them.
- Talking to people is not enough; we should always explain how we will respond or use the views expressed.

DIG DEEPER

Focusing on outcomes A focus on achieving improved outcomes for children, young people and their families is a major part of the Every Child Matters agenda.

The Outcomes Framework is organised into five broad areas of improvement as an aim for all children's lives: staying safe, being healthy, achieving economic well-being, enjoying and achieving, and making a positive contribution. Within each of these five areas, the framework sets out many aspects of children's lives that can be measured so that improved outcomes can be demonstrated.

See Every Child Matters website – the Outcomes Framework www.everychildmatters.gov.uk/aims/outcomes
Children's Workforce Development Council: *Guidance on Common assessment framework, lead professional, common core of skills and knowledge and one workforce framework*
www.cwdcouncil.org.uk/caf

Children's Workforce Development Council – CWDC Share! Emerging practice in integrated working
www.cwdcouncil.org.uk/cwdc-share

Every Child Matters Common Core of skills and Knowledge
www.everychildmatters.gov.uk/deliveringservices/commoncore/

Hear by Right toolkit http://hbr.nya.org.uk/resources/disability_toolkit

Friedman M (2005) *Trying Hard is Not Good Enough: How to produce measurable improvements for customers and communities.* Trafford Publishing
This book is about 'getting from talk to action quickly'. It aims to provide a method of thinking and taking action that is simple, common sense and useful to community members, managers and decision makers.

Here are some practical things you can do...

...to engage with service users

'Work with young people to design a website.'

'Use Viewpoint – it's a useful interactive questionnaire.'

'Be clear about what can be influenced and be sure to go back and say what has happened to the views and suggestions made.'

'Help parents, carers and children and young people to be confident in assessing service quality and gathering views themselves. Show you value people by providing the funding for these activities.'

'Use advocates and independent chairing of reviews.'

'Collect service user feedback on an individual basis and from groups.'

'Review your service by collecting service users' views.'

'Make sure ad hoc feedback regarding service delivery is passed back to management – and that it is responded to!'

'Provide a suggestions box.'

Governance – support from senior managers and decision makers

The Audit Commission defines corporate governance in the public sector as:

> *the framework of accountability to users, stakeholders and the wider community, within which organisations take decisions, and lead and control their functions, to achieve their objectives.*
>
> (Audit Commission website)

Research has noted that if effective governance is not in place, there will be an impact on time, capacity and morale.

> *The potential for teams to be distracted from their core tasks by the time spent on resolving management structures was significant. Practical problems concerning differences in pay, leave entitlements and freedom to make decisions without referral to line managers caused real problems for team members and their managers who reported an adverse effect on morale.*
>
> (Anning et al, 2006)

Children and Young People's Trust Boards are the major vehicle for the strategic planning and local delivery of the Every Child Matters agenda. It is their task to ensure there is appropriate governance for integrated working.

> *Partnerships should be hosted within Children's Trust arrangements as a major plank of implementation.*
>
> (Every Child Matters website)

Frost's review identified basic requirements for successful integrated working including the need for all agencies with staff involved to:

- *develop formal structures for liaison with other agencies responsible for the multiagency team and agree collectively how the team and its members will be managed*
- *provide clarity about the aims and objectives of the team if the team are to organise themselves to deliver those objectives.*

(Frost, 2005)

This implies a joint approach to the way that integrated practice will be operated. In Chapter 5 (in the section on 'structural issues – systems and management'), we focused on how practitioners and their immediate managers experience structures and management arrangements. But this will also need action and attention from the management hierarchy above those who manage the front line.

In other words, these are issues that need to be addressed in the governance of the integrated services we are addressing here. Those governance structures, ie the Children and Young People's Trust, need to ensure that collective agreements are drawn up, implemented and reviewed. The Lead Member for Children's Services and the Director of Children's Services have responsibilities executed through the Children and Young People's Trust Board.

eg

Engaging peripheral team members

By using the Tools in this Handbook, one authority found that front-line staff were not aware of how their work linked to the wider Children and Young People's plan for their area and the structures that supported its delivery. (This authority had considered itself to be well advanced towards achieving integrated services.) The manager was able to see the value of showing staff those plans and working with them to see their own role in their delivery. (The diagram on integrated working featured in the introductory section of this Handbook was part of that communication process.)

And here are some practical things you can do...

...to ensure effective governance

'Terms of reference of strategic bodies or management groups should include identification of risks, contingency plans and dispute resolution procedures.'

'There should be an annual review against objectives and robust joint working agreements.'

'Meetings should be effectively planned and managed.'

'Spell out the roles and responsibilities of integrated practice leaders/ co-ordinators and managers, and senior managers through to the board or steering group. Make sure that concerns and successes have a route to be reported and celebrated or resolved.'

'It was difficult; we felt no one was interested. There were particular problems with differences in pay and terms and conditions of employment. Then suddenly there was national interest and everyone wanted to own the project.'

'We have lots of joint procedures, multiagency panels, but it's difficult to make progress when there is so much other change and funding is restricted or cut back.'

eg

Achieving change through using governance structures

In a joint police and social care team, a detective inspector who had been a champion for partnership working left. The new link came from a lower rank. This led to concerns within the team that the initiative would no longer receive as much attention and support. Project staff took their concerns to the top of their own organisations. The police did see themselves as having a key role to play and realised they should not have made such a decision without reference to partners. Following further discussion, it was agreed that the police would ensure the link manager was of an appropriate rank, matched to other organisations. This felt like a good resolution.

DIG DEEPER

Dig deeper for resources about governance...

Percy–Smith J (2005) *What Works in Strategic Partnerships for Children?* Barkingside: Barnardo's

Every Child Matters website – provides 'models for governance'
www.everychildmatters.gov.uk/deliveringservices/multiagencyworking/managerstoolkit/strategicpartners/governance/
and 'easy tasks for a steering group'.
www.everychildmatters.gov.uk/deliveringservices/multiagencyworking/managerstoolkit/buildingtheworkgroup/

Children's Workforce Development Council – one workforce framework and tools to support authorities in assessing progress on Children and Young People's Trusts
http://onechildrensworkforce.cwdcouncil.org.uk/walkthrough/framework

Measuring progress – building in evaluation

It is important to evaluate your new way of working, and to be able to show change effected in the lives of children and young people. This will help in building the evidence base for your work and in making the case for support and funding to become secure.

All local authorities are subject to a performance regime that measures and reports on progress and quality in children's services. Performance reports and ratings for all authorities are posted on the Every Child Matters website.

The changing way that inspections have been carried out has reflected the focus on effective joining up of services to deliver improved outcomes in partnership with parents and children and young people. From 2005 to 2008 services were monitored through two inspection processes: an annual performance assessment (APA) of each council's children's services, and a programme of joint area reviews (JARs), which range beyond council services to include, for example, health and police services. Both processes looked at how services were working together locally to improve outcomes for children and young people.

From 2009, APAs will be replaced by a new inspection system: the Comprehensive Area Assessment (CAA), which will ensure a stronger focus on front-line practice, including annual unannounced inspection visits in every local authority to complement a three-year, more intensive programme of inspection. The targets and indicators for your local authority will be publicised through the Children and Young People's Plan in your area. If you look at that as a team, you will be able to see how your work supports the local vision for children and young people and what measures are being used to capture progress.

The kinds of outcome you might be able to measure are listed in a publication from the National College for School Leadership:

- improved co-ordination of services
- improved quality of life
- better and quicker access to services
- reduced stress felt by service users
- feeling involved or listened to and not having to tell the story over and over
- more appropriate services for the child and their family
- reduced need for specialist services.

(Coleman, 2006)

4

See what the Change Project Group had to say about outcomes for service users. Watch the fourth film on the videoCD.

The evaluation report of the Local Authorities Research Consortium (Lord et al, 2008) also distinguishes levels of outcome and gives examples, based on a four-stage model of impact that suggests different levels of impact over time.

If you are collecting any such information, you will need to start with some benchmarking so you can demonstrate change.

And here are some practical things you can do...

...to measure the impact of integrated working on service users

TOOL 11

Doing things differently
Tool 11 is a log that you can use to capture the outcomes of integrated working– both in terms of positive outcomes and areas for learning.

'Undertake research to see if outcomes are changing.'

'Produce regular management reports.'

'Bring together the management reports from different agencies involved in joint working.'

'Compare attendance rates, behaviour logs.'

'Ask teachers to comment on kids' progress in school.'

'Ask parent(s) to comment on progress.'

'Record and observe changes in performance indicators.'

DIG DEEPER

Assessing performance

Dig deeper for these important documents and websites........

Every Child Matters: The Framework for the Inspection of Children's Services. A strategic document of interest to senior officers and managers of services for children and young people. Available from www.ofsted.gov.uk

Children's Services inspection www.everychildmatters.gov.uk/strategy/inspection/

DCSF, The Childrens Plan: Building brighter futures: Next steps for the Children's Workforce www.dcsf.gov.uk/childrensplan/ DCSF, 2020 Children and young people's workforce strategy DCSF www.everychildmatters.gov.uk/deliveringservices/childrenandyoungpeoplesworkforce/
Coleman A (2006) Collaborative Leadership in Extended Schools: Leading in a multiagency environment. Nottingham: National College for School Leadership (NCSL)
Online version available at www.ncsl.org.uk/media/56A/55/collaborative-leadership-in-extended-schools.pdf

Local Authorities Research Consortium www.nfer.ac.uk/research-areas/pims-data/summaries/larc.cfm

research in practice (second edition, 2005) NIFTY: An introductory Handbook for social care staff with a rough guide to evaluation resources. (Small-scale evaluation for single services) www.rip.org.uk/nifty

7
Maintaining momentum

Maintaining momentum

This chapter makes some practical suggestions for ensuring that you continue to move forward and review what you have learned.

If you have worked through this Handbook using some or all of the Tools, then you will now have a lot of information about integrated practice that you are involved in. In particular, the questionnaires (Tools 4-7) linked to the four themes should have given you a score for each section and an overall score. You will also have set out ways in which you can address low scores. We suggest that you now:

- build these suggestions into an action plan
- establish a regular process for reviewing progress on the action plan
- and set a time – perhaps six months to a year ahead – to assess your work again using the Tools in this Handbook.

You can also report on your findings to senior managers in the agencies involved or to your Children and Young People's Trust if appropriate. When compiling such a report, it's important to identify WHO needs to do WHAT to achieve the action plan. In particular, you should highlight:

- actions that require support or action by those other than front-line managers
- any resources that may be needed to support action
- the improvements you expect to see as a result of taking the action forward
- and the ways you will measure change that occurs.

Action plan
You are most likely to make progress with integrated working if you break down the tasks you have to do into small steps and then identify the actions you need to take for each step. Many action plans fail because the tasks appear too difficult. You may have several goals but you need to break each down into a list of tasks. Set a timescale for each action, but be realistic – do not expect the impossible.

It will also help if you link your actions to the Children and Young People's Plan and, through that, to local and national targets and indicators. In this way you can see the contribution of your team in a wider context.

And in conclusion

We hope you have found this Handbook valuable. The Handbook is the result of three years' work but, as we emphasise throughout, the changes set out in Every Child Matters will inevitably take considerable time. This is why we have suggested you develop an action plan and return to it to check progress every six months or so.

This Handbook is one of a number of guides or tools to support the development of integrated working. However, it is unique in its focus on working on the front line and the presentation of research evidence. Through the **research in practice** Change Project process, it has also been possible to record the feelings of some of those involved in practice and the suggestions they have made, which draw on their experience of what works.

research in practice will continue to report and summarise new research in this area. Hopefully all of you who use this Handbook will continue to see the value of using research and will follow developments in integrated practice. If we are to achieve improved outcomes for children and young people, we do need to understand how to work together effectively and to develop ways of working built on that knowledge.

References and where to find out more

Anning A, Cottrell D, Frost N, Green J and Robinson M (2006) *Developing Multiprofessional Teamwork for Integrated Children's Services.* Maidenhead: Open University Press

Audit Commission (2004) Youth Justice 2004: *A review of the reformed youth justice system.* London: Audit Commission

Barnardo's (2005) *Meeting with Respect Resource Pack.*

Beecham J and Sinclair I (2007) *Costs and Outcomes in Children's Social Care: Messages from research.* London: Jessica Kingsley Publishers
Online version available at www.everychildmatters.gov.uk/resources-and-practice/RS00026

Blewett J, Lewis J and Tunstill J (2007) *The Changing Roles and Tasks of Social Work: A Literature Informed Discussion Paper.* London: General Social Care Council

Boddy J, Simon A and Wigfall V (2007) *Evaluation of a Link Social Worker Post in Two Islington Children's Centres.* London: Thomas Coram Research Unit, Institute of Education, University of London

Bowyer S (2008a) Improving Outcomes for children – Community Care 22.5.08- (Referring to ;-Lord P, Kinder K, Atkinson M and Harland J Evaluating the Early Impact of integrated Children's Services (2008) LARC (Local Authority Research Consortium) www.nfer.ac.uk/larc

Bowyer S (2008b) Prompt 3. *Multi-professional Working: Distinct professional identities in multi-professional teams.* **research in practice** web-based review Available online at www.rip.org.uk/prompts

Carpenter J and Dickinson H (2008) *Interprofessional Education and Training.* Bristol: The Policy Press (in association with Community Care as part of the Better Partnership Working series)

Children's Workforce Development Council (2004) *Sector Qualifications Strategies: A guide to development and implementation.* Leeds: CWDC
Online version available at www.cwdcouncil.org.uk/sector-learning-strategy

Children's Workforce Network (2009) *Integrated Qualifications Framework*
Available online at www.iqf.org.uk

Coleman A (2006) *Collaborative Leadership in Extended Schools: Leading in a multiagency environment.* Nottingham: National College for School Leadership
Online version available at www.ncsl.org.uk/media/56A/55/collaborative-leadership-in-extended-schools.pdf

Council for Disabled Children/Contact a Family (2004) *Parent Participation: Improving services for disabled children.* Professionals' guide. London: Contact a Family/Council for Disabled Children
Online version available at www.cafamily.org.uk/ContactProf05.pdf

Daniels H, Edwards A, Creese A, Leadbetter J and Martin D (2008) *Learning in and for Interagency Working: Non-technical summary (research summary). ESRC End of award report, RES-139-25-0100-A.* Swindon: Economic and Social Research Council

Department for Children, Schools and Families (2007a) *The Children's Plan: Building brighter futures.* London: TSO (The Stationery Office) (Cm 7280)
Online version available at www.dcsf.gov.uk/childrensplan

Department for Children, Schools and Families (2007b) *Effective Integrated Working: Findings of Concept of Operations Study. Integrated working to improve outcomes for children and young people.* London: DCSF
Online version available at www.everychildmatters.gov.uk/resources-and-practice/IG00260

Department for Children, Schools and Families (2008a) *2020 Children and Young People's Workforce Strategy.* Nottingham: DCSF
Online version available at
www.everychildmatters.gov.uk/deliveringservices/childrenandyoungpeoplesworkforce/

Department for Children, Schools and Families (2008b) *Building Brighter Futures: Next steps for the children's workforce.* Nottingham: DCSF
Online version available at
http://publications.teachernet.gov.uk/eOrderingDownload/DCSF-00292-2008.pdf

Department for Education and Skills (1998) *Excellence for All Children: Meeting special educational needs.* London: HMSO
Online version available at
www.teachernet.gov.uk/wholeschool/sen/publications/excellencegp

Department for Education and Skills (2003) *Every Child Matters.* London: Stationery Office (Cm 5860)
Online version available at www.everychildmatters.gov.uk/aims/background

Department for Education and Skills (2004) *Every Child Matters: The next steps.* Nottingham: DfES Publications
Online version available at
www.dcsf.gov.uk/consultations/downloadableDocs/EveryChildMattersNextSteps.pdf

Department for Education and Skills (2005) *Every Child Matters: Common Core of Skills and Knowledge*
www.everychildmatters.gov.uk/deliveringservices/commoncore/

Department for Education and Skills (2006) *Championing Children: A shared set of skills, knowledge and behaviours for those leading and managing integrated children's services.* London: Stationery Office
www.everychildmatters.gov.uk/_files/Championing%20Children%20Single%20Pg.pdf

Edwards A, Daniels H, Gallagher T, Leadbetter J and Warmington P (2009) *Improving Inter-professional Collaborations: Multi-agency working for children's well-being*. London and New York: Routledge

Ellis T and Boden I (2005) *Is there a Unifying Professional Culture in Youth Offending Teams?* London: British Society of Criminology

Engeström Y (2000) 'Activity Theory as a Framework for Analyzing and Redesigning Work' *Ergonomics* 43 (7)

Friedman M (2005) *Trying Hard is Not Good Enough: How to produce measurable improvements for customers and communities*. Trafford Publishing

Frost N (2005) *Professionalism, Partnership and Joined-up Thinking: A research review of front-line working with children and families*. Dartington: **research in practice**
Online version available at www.rip.org.uk/publications/researchreviews.asp

Glasby J and Dickinson H (2008) *Partnership Working in Health and Social Care*. Bristol: The Policy Press (in association with Community Care as part the Better Partnership Working series)

Hodson R and Cooke E (2007) *Leading Evidence-Informed Practice: A Handbook*. Dartington: **research in practice**
Online version available at
www.rip.org.uk/publications/handbook_detail.asp?pub_id=40

Home Office (1998) 'Interdepartmental Circular on Establishing Youth Offending Teams' 22 December. London: Home Office
Online version available at
www.nationalarchives.gov.uk/ERORecords/HO/421/2/cdact/yotcirc2.htm

Laming H (2003) *The Victoria Climbié Inquiry*. London: Stationery Office
Online version available at
http://www.victoria-climbie-inquiry.org.uk/finreport/finreport.htm

Lewin K (1951) *Field Theory in Social Sciences*. New York: Harper & Row

Lord P, Kinder K, Wilkin A, Atkinson M and Harland J (2008) *Evaluating the Early Impact of Integrated Children's Services*. Round 1 Final Report. Slough: NFER
Online version available at www.nfer.ac.uk/research-areas/pims-data/summaries/larc.cfm

Moran P, Jacobs C, Bunn A and Bifulco A (2007) 'Multi-agency Working: Implications for an early-intervention social work team' *Child & Family Social Work* 12 (2)

Morrow G, Malin N and Jennings T (2005) 'Interprofessional Teamworking for Child and Family Referral in a Sure Start Local Programme' *Journal of Interprofessional Care* 19 (2)

NHS Health Advisory Service (1995) *Child and Adolescent Mental Health Services: Together We Stand.* London: HAS

Ovretveit J (1993) *Coordinating Community Care: Multidisciplinary teams and care management.* Buckingham/Philadelphia: Open University Press

Percy–Smith J (2005) *What Works in Strategic Partnerships for Children?* Barkingside: Barnardo's

Shaw C (2005) *NIFTY Evaluation: An introductory Handbook for social care staff with a rough guide to evaluation resources.* Dartington: research in practice
Online version available at www.rip.org.uk/nifty

Social Care Institute for Excellence (2006) *Practice Guide 6: Involving Children and Young People in Developing Social Care.*
Online version available at
www.scie.org.uk/publications/guides/guide11/index.asp

Warmington P, Daniels H, Edwards A, Leadbetter J, Martin D, Brown S and Middleton D (2004a) 'Conceptualising Professional Learning for Multi-Agency Working and User Engagement'. British Educational Research Association Annual Conference, UMIST Manchester.
Online version available at http://en.scientificcommons.org/8677436

Warmington P, Daniels H, Edwards A, Leadbetter J, Martin D, Brown S and Middleton D (2004b) 'Learning in and for interagency working: conceptual tensions in 'joined up' practice.' TLRP Annual Conference, Cardiff.

Wenger E (1998) *Communities of Practice: Learning, meaning and identity.* Cambridge: Cambridge University Press

White S and Featherstone B (2005) 'Communicating Misunderstandings: Multi-agency work as social practice' *Child and Family Social Work* 10 (3)

Websites

You may also find these websites particularly useful.

Centre for Excellence and Outcomes in Children and Young People's Services (C4EO) www.c4eo.org.uk

The Children Act (2004)
www.opsi.gov.uk/ACTS/acts2004/en/ukpgaen_20040031_en_1

Children's Services Inspection
www.everychildmatters.gov.uk/strategy/inspection/

Children's Trusts www.everychildmatters.gov.uk/aims/childrenstrusts/

Children's Workforce Development Council: one workforce framework and tools to support authorities in assessing www.cwdcouncil.org.uk/

The Children's Workforce Network www.childrensworkforce.org.uk/

Early Support www.earlysupport.org.uk
Here you will find access to a range of practical materials published by the Department for Children, Schools and Families to support the government's Early Support programme, including an audit tool.

Every Child Matters website – provides 'models for governance'
www.everychildmatters.gov.uk/deliveringservices/multiagencyworking/managerstoolkit/strategicpartners/governance/

Every Child Matters: Change for Children – Setting up multiagency services
www.everychildmatters.gov.uk/deliveringservices/multiagencyworking
These pages of the Every Child Matters website provide information and guidance about multiagency services, including online toolkits for practitioners and managers.

Every Child Matters: 'easy tasks for a steering group'.
www.everychildmatters.gov.uk/deliveringservices/multiagencyworking/managerstoolkit/buildingtheworkgroup/

Every Child Matters: The Framework for the Inspection of Children's Services. A strategic document of interest to senior officers and managers of services for children and young people. Available from www.ofsted.gov.uk

Guidance on Children's and Young People's Plan
www.everychildmatters.gov.uk/strategy/guidance/

Hear By Right www.nya.org.uk/hearbyright
This National Youth Agency website offers a standards framework for organisations across the statutory and voluntary sectors to assess and improve practice and policy on the active involvement of children and young people.

Local Authorities Research Consortium (LARC)
www.nfer.ac.uk/research-areas/pims-data/summaries/larc.cfm

Ready Steady Change www.crae.org.uk
These web pages from the Children's Rights Alliance for England contains a range of materials and guidance designed to help put children and young people's wishes, feelings and ideas at the centre of public services.

National Foundation for Educational Research www.nfer.ac.uk

research in practice www.rip.org.uk

r u OK? Website www.ru-ok.org.uk/

All website addresses checked April 2009

Tools

This section of the Handbook contains all the Tools refered to in the previous chapters. Electronic copies of these Tools (in PDF format) are also contained on the CD inside the back flap for you to print off as plain A4 sheets. You might use the column of boxes to tick off the ones you've used.

1. ☐ Opportunities and threats
2. ☐ Understanding your team
3. ☐ How joined up are you?
4. ☐ Checklist: Structural issues – systems and management
5. ☐ Checklist: Ideological frameworks – sharing and redistributing knowledge, skills and beliefs
6. ☐ Checklist: Procedural influences – participation in developing new processes
7. ☐ Checklist: Interprofessional learning – through role change
8. ☐ Are we making a difference? Focus on outcomes
9. ☐ Exploring attitudes and beliefs
10. ☐ Common Core of Skills and Knowledge
11. ☐ Doing things differently
12. ☐ Using common language
13. ☐ Speed dating – getting to know you
14. ☐ Action plan

6

See how the people in the pilot group used the Tools to improve their integrated working. Listen to what they have to say about the impact they had on their work.

Responsibilities Who is going to take responsibility for actions?	**Timescale** When will each action be achieved?	**Measure** How will you know it has been achieved? What is the evidence? What are your measures?	**Outcome** What will change? Who will benefit?

Action plan

You are most likely to make progress with integrated working if you break down the tasks you have to do into small steps and then identify the actions you need to take for each step. Many action plans fail because the tasks appear too difficult. You may have several goals, but you need to break each down into a list of tasks. Set a timescale for each action, but be realistic – do not expect the impossible.

First, as a group, identify clear and specific goals and what the outcome will be. Then identify:

- what actions you will take
- who is going to take responsibility for each action
- when each action will be achieved
- how you know it will have been achieved.

When you have completed the plan, distribute copies to all members of the team. Bring copies to meetings to review and update regularly.

Aim/Vision/Goal What do you want to achieve?	**Actions** What are you g do to achieve t

Adapted from Basildon West's integrated wor

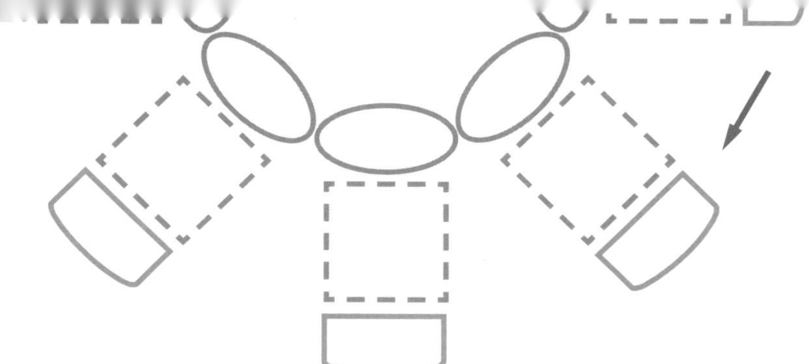

2 Before starting, decide as a group two things you would like to know about each other, for example:.

- Q What skills and experience do you each bring to your team?
- Q What does your colleague do in an average day?

3
- Allow 10 minutes (5 minutes each) for each pair to get as much information as they can from each other.
- Ring a bell, blow a whistle or shout when that 10 minutes is up; those in the outer circle must then move on to the next person.
- Then get the outer circles to swap tables and start again.

4 When you've finished, get together as a group and see if any particular themes have emerged – and if any action is needed.

TOOL 12 Use this exercise in conjunction with Tool 12 Using common language

Adapted from exercise devised by Peter Fanshawe, Wiltshire County Council

Speed dating – getting to know you

People in multiprofessional teams interact differently – using different language or drawing on distinct expertise according to their unique professional experience. Different training backgrounds are evident in the diverse approaches that practitioners might take to aspects of their work and current problems faced by children and their families. This 'speed dating' exercise may help to dispel some of the differences that might be encountered and will certainly help you get to know more about each other's approach.

How to do this exercise

This is an exercise that could usefully be used at a team away day, or a locality team meeting. It needs plenty of time to work well. Inevitably there will not necessarily be time to explore everything, but that is the nature of speed dating!

1

- Set out two circles of small tables with two chairs on opposite sides
- Leave room for privacy – it could get quite noisy
- People in the inner circle should stay in their seats
- The outer circle should be the ones to circulate

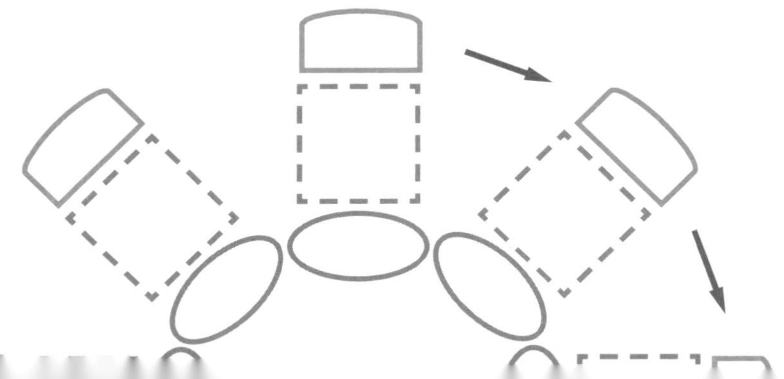

	[illegible] refers to children and young persons' rather than youth	
eg child care	• looked after children, child protection services and family support services (children's services) • nurseries, crèches, childminders, and out-of-hours care in schools (schools / general public) • government's strategy for childcare (2004) covers maternity leave and financial support for parents	
eg case conference	• a formal meeting involving a wide range of practitioners and a child and their family, held when a child is thought to be at continuing risk of significant harm (children's services) • a professional meeting at which clinicians present the details of a case to their peers as an aid to training and professional development (the child or young person's family may also attend the case conference) (health)	

As a group, discuss the difficulties that these differences can cause. Discuss whether there are common themes emerging. Are the differences greater or less than expected? Can you agree on any shared terms?

See Multi-agency Working: Glossary at www.everychildmatters.gov.uk/deliveringservices/multiagencyworking/glossary/
This was produced by DfES for managers and practitioners from different backgrounds working in multiagency settings to promote and facilitate communication and understanding.

your definitions

General term	Different interpretations of the same term	Preferred, shared or agreed term

TOOL 12

Using common language

People say that the lack of a common language is one of the key barriers to effective integrated practice.

How to use this Tool

Use this Tool to explain core terms and definitions that can be interpreted differently by practitioners working in a multiagency setting and so lead to misunderstandings between different professions. As a group, try to bring together and explain the overlap between different words that are used by different agencies to explain similar things. The Tool will provide a starting point for you to consider how you use terms appropriately and where you could reduce the use of jargon and acronyms. It may raise your awareness as a team about terms that are falling out of use and other terms that are preferred, together with the reasons for this. Practitioners need to be very specific when completing common assessments, for example – while also considering how to ensure the language is accessible to all.

In multiagency groups try to come up with at least five examples of how the different agencies in your team have different meanings for similar terms.

General term	Different interpretations of the same term	Preferred, shared or agreed term
eg at risk	• at risk – of significant harm and therefore in need of protection by local authority (children's services) • at risk – of social exclusion (schools) • at risk – of offending (youth justice)	
eg youth	• 13-19 age group, as in youth green paper (government)	

			… achieving positive outcomes • Time saving – on phone calls • Would be helpful if PA for LAC was situated in Locality Team Improved understanding of each others' roles example
			your incident

NB if you use this Tool for training purposes remember the importance of keeping a child or young person's identity confidential.

6		
7		
8		

Adapted from a Locality Team evaluation. The team comprises social workers, family support workers, an education welfare officer, a Connexions PA, a transitions support worker, an education psychologist and an administrative support team.

TOOL 11

Doing things differently

Personal log

Use this log to reflect on what you think has worked well in your team. What are the benefits of integrated working for you as a front-line practitioner and for the children and young people you work with?

This can be reviewed regularly in supervision and will give you a personal perspective on the wider benefits of integrated working. (This personal log can inform any records about positive outcomes kept by the team.)

	Date	Action taken
1	Jan 05	Attended multidisciplinary meeting and was able to sort a lot of issues with children. Enabled knowledge/understanding of different professional roles.
2	Feb 05	Multidisciplinary meeting re troublesome teenagers. Education Welfare Officer provided knowledge to Fieldwork Manager enabling FWM to challenge school representatives to take responsibility for teenagers.
3		
4		

example

TOOL 11

Doing things differently

Use these logs to capture and reflect on the outcomes of integrated working (both in terms of positive outcomes and areas for learning).

Team log

Set an agenda item in team meetings to record and reflect on significant events.
Keep a log of positive outcomes of meetings, action taken, who was present and the agencies involved.
This log (example below) may help to:

- improve communication between disciplines
- reduce duplication
- increase the time spent working with your client group.

Date	Child or young person's unique reference	Agencies involved in this meeting	Action taken
Jan 05		Connexions/ Family Support Worker/ CP	Best outcome achieved because staff had access to support from colleagues from other disciplines and therefore made better informed decision (Individual) Re-referrals prevented Consistent message/experience to young people, family and professionals
Feb 05		Transitions Support [illegible]	Advice sought by TSW from SW in respect of seeking support from other agencies • Sharing knowledge/resources

TOOL 1

Opportunities and threats[1]

Use this Tool to identify those factors that, from a practitioner's point of view, will help drive integrated practice - and those factors that will restrain its progress. Use it to help you find sources of support for the process of integrated working – and to identify those things that might get in the way.

1. Do this exercise individually first. Try to identify the opportunities you think will particularly help integrated practice. Then think about the threats that might hinder progress. What might threaten your team's chances of achieving its aims?
2. Then draw the diagram on a flip chart and complete it as a group. (You could start with your own professional group and compare results with another professional group in your integrated team – but be mindful of issues that might be sensitive such as trust, safety, different professional values, or local issues.)

Indicate the strength of the force by the thickness of the arrow.

Opportunities

Opportunities might include shared aims and values, involving everyone, and wanting to get on with working together.

Threats

Professional attitudes and values, lack of acceptance that there is another way of doing things, division and rivalry and different models of explanation (ie 'social' or 'medical' models) can act as significant threats to better integrated working.

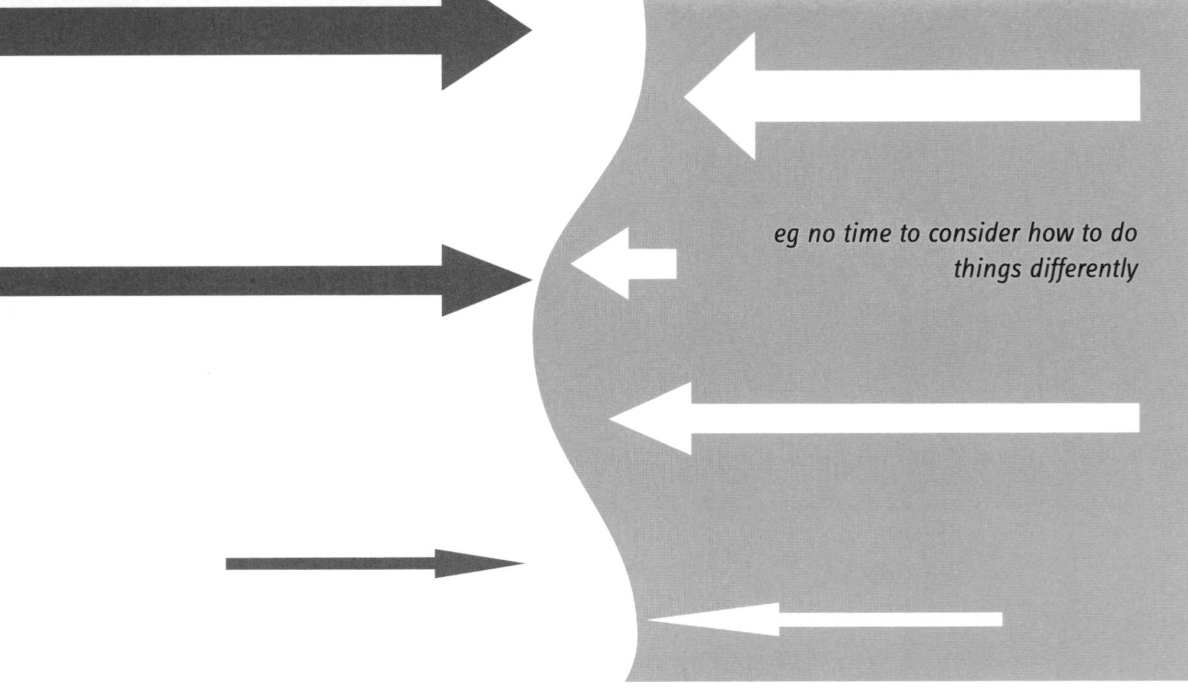

- Look at the threats and see how they can be removed, reduced or avoided – make a list of suggestions
- Look at the opportunities and see how you can build on these – make a list of suggestions

If you act on these ideas, are the opportunities together likely to outweigh the threats?

[1]Adapted from: Lewin K (1951) *Field Theory in Social Sciences*. Harper and Row

TOOL 2

Understanding your team

The three sections to this Tool should help you understand how integrated practice is delivered where you are working. The diagrams you produce here could be useful for showing new staff how the team works, or for explaining in a clear way to service users who is who and how the service works. It is helpful to have your plans for the team available for this exercise so that members can understand how they impact on those plans.

The three sections cover:

1. the range of practitioners in your team and how they are managed
2. different agencies who have contributed to the team
3. exploring boundaries – how your team links to other agencies and reflecting on how to improve those links.

(Examples of diagrams supplement those given elsewhere in the Handbook)

1. The range of workers in your team and how they are managed

Produce a diagram showing:

- the range of practitioners from differing professional backgrounds in your integrated team
- how they are each managed, supervised and co-ordinated.

Differentiate the ways they are managed by using solid and dotted lines

Line management

Co-ordination

2. Different agencies who have contributed to the team – employment structure

Produce a diagram to show the different agencies who have contributed to the team and the nature of that contribution.

Show part-time staff and the fact that some agencies are linked but do not contribute staff time.

- Use different colours to denote different agencies.
- Represent practitioners with small circles.
- Use a larger circle to show what part of a contributing agency is 'within' the team and what without.

Example b:

Head Injury Team: Employment Structure

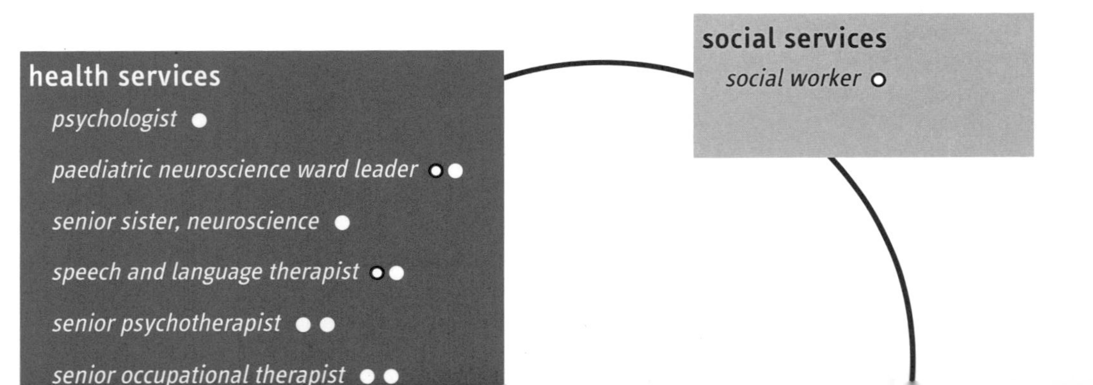

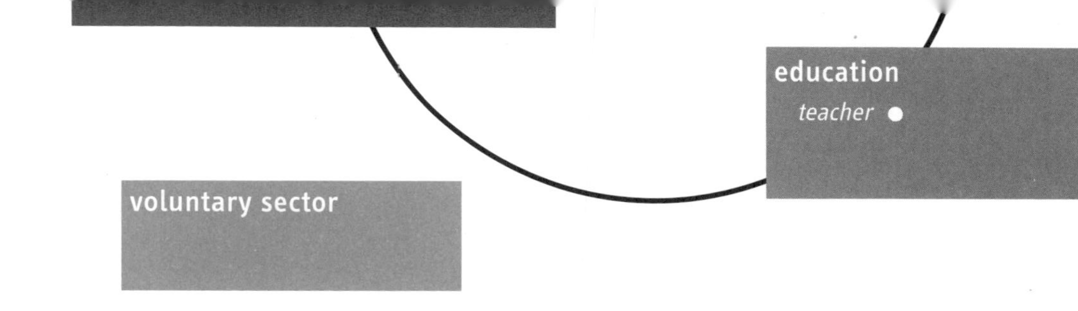

Key
Full time ●
Part time ○

This tool is adapted from Anning A et al (2006) *Developing Multi-professional Teamwork for Integrated Children's Services*, using Ovretveit's framework - in Ovretveit J (1993) *Coordinating Community Care: Multi-disciplinary Teams and Care Management*. Buckingham: Open University Press - and a model of integrated working provided by Telford and Wrekin.

Example a: Head injury team – how staff are managed

Head Injury Team Management Structure

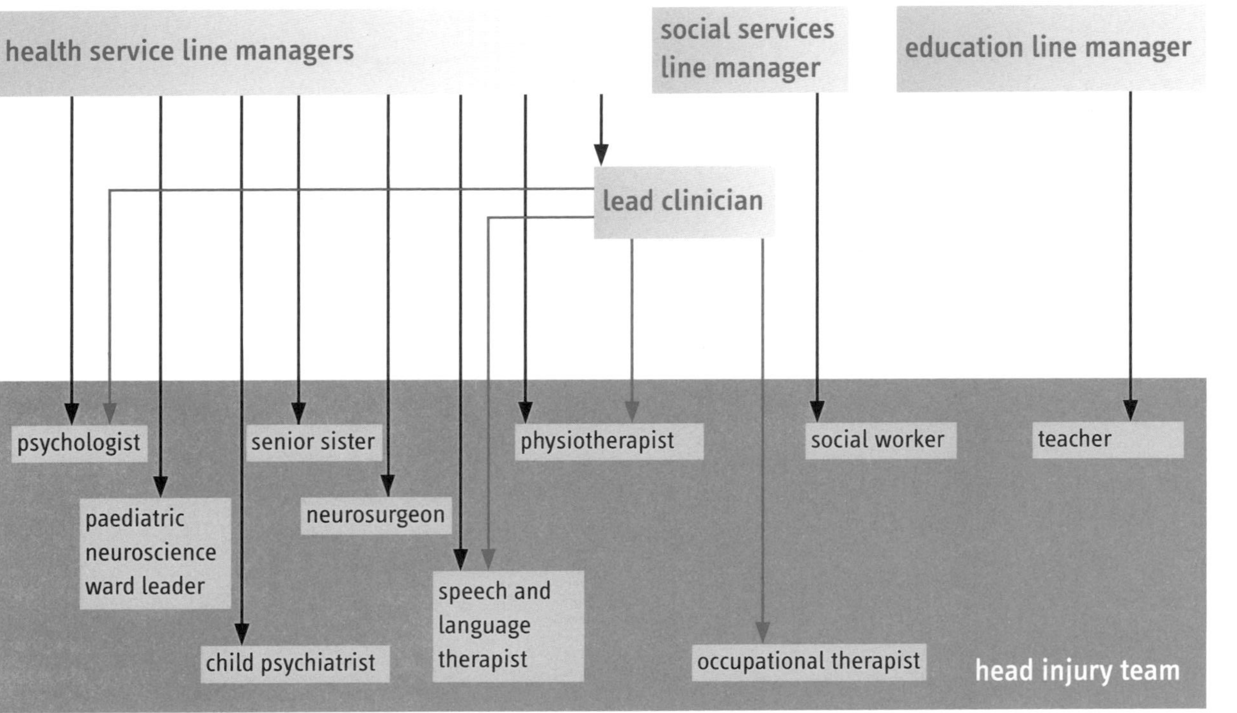

This tool is adapted from Anning A et al (2006) *Developing Multi-professional Teamwork for Integrated Children's Services*, using Ovretveit's framework - in Ovretveit J (1993) *Coordinating Community Care: Multi-disciplinary Teams and Care Management*. Buckingham: Open University Press - and a model of integrated working provided by Telford and Wrekin.

TOOL 2

3. Exploring boundaries– how your team links to other agencies

The example below shows the complexity of the relationships and boundaries between agencies, individuals and teams in an integrated working model. Creating an integrated team generates new boundaries with a range of organisations. It is important to pay as much attention to the boundaries as it is to the core. (Wenger, 1998)

Draw a similar map of your organisation and how it relates to organisations it borders on. Some boundaries might be liquid and fluid, others might be more rigid and difficult to penetrate.

Represent proximity by distance, conflict by crossed lines, good relationships by strong lines etc. You can then identify where conflict or lack of relationship is blocking progress and make an action plan to resolve this.

See Tool 14
Action plan

Example c:

Integrated working in Telford and Wrekin

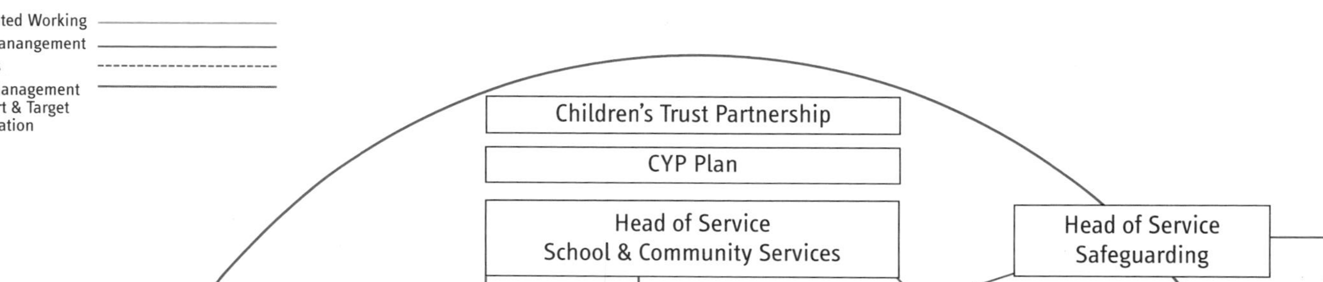

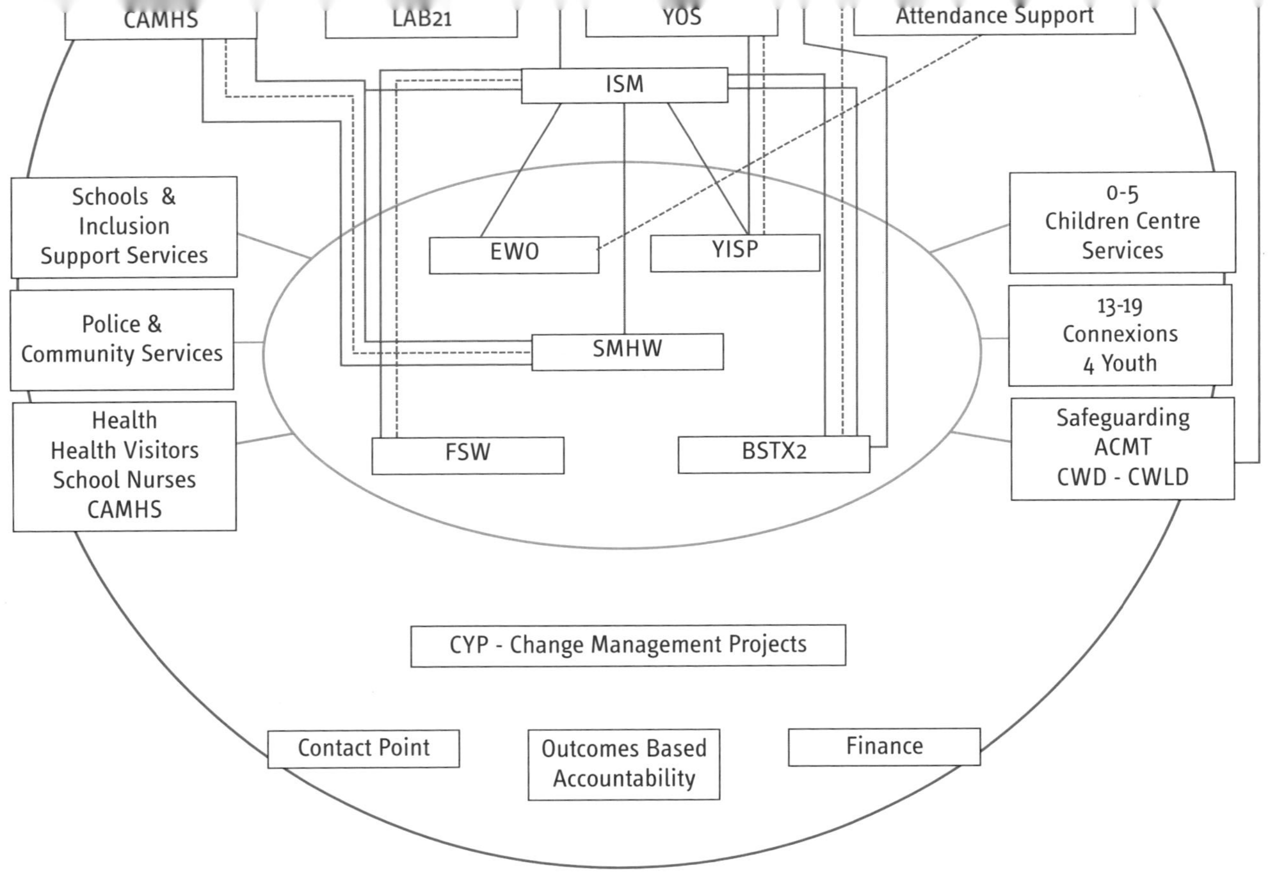

This tool is adapted from Anning A et al (2006) *Developing Multi-professional Teamwork for Integrated Children's Services*, using Ovretveit's framework - in Ovretveit J (1993) *Coordinating Community Care: Multi-disciplinary Teams and Care Management*. Buckingham: Open University Press - and a model of integrated working provided by Telford and Wrekin.

TOOL 3

How joined up are you?

Use this Tool to describe the model of integrated practice where you are.

Where would you place your team on this continuum? What are you working toward? Use this to explore ideas and feelings about becoming an integrated team. You may find that some services work alongside you under the same manager while others stand outside that arrangement.

You can carry out this exercise as an individual and/or as a team. Use it to plot where you are as an integrated team. It can highlight whether managers are managing and communicating the integrated vision or not and whether all services are engaged, and also how aware individuals are of the objectives of the integration. Be careful though. It can unearth unseen dynamics as well as highlighting how people feel and whether staff anxieties have been managed. If different members of the same integrated team place themselves in different places discuss the reasons.

Try using this Tool at an away day or at a locality team meeting.

Level of integration					**where we are now** ✓	**where we want to be** ✓
merger/ integration	Services work together toward consistent goals and complementary services, while maintaining their	Services plan together and address issues of overlap, duplication and gaps in service provision toward common	Services work together in a planned and systematic manner toward shared and agreed goals	Different services become one organisation in order to enhance service delivery		

co-ordination	Services work together toward consistent goals and complementary services, while maintaining their independence	Services plan together and address issues of overlap, duplication and gaps in service provision toward common outcomes	Services work together in a planned and systematic manner toward shared and agreed goals				
collaboration	Services work together toward consistent goals and complementary services, while maintaining their independence	Services plan together and address issues of overlap, duplication and gaps in service provision toward common outcomes					
co-operation	Services work together toward consistent goals and complementary services, while maintaining their independence						

Adapted from the London Borough of Merton's Ladder of Partnership (2008) and Frost N (2005) *Professionalism, Partnership and joined-up Thinking: a research review of front-line working with children and families.* Dartington: **research in practice**

TOOL 4

Checklist: Structural issues – systems and management

This checklist will help you decide where to focus your efforts to achieve effective integrated practice.

Structural issues - systems and management		If 'yes' how do you know this? What have you done?	If 'no' what action could you take?
Research tip (Frost, 2005): Procedures and policies only become real on the front line, so effective integrated working requires procedures that have been developed with the participation of front-line staff. This takes time, careful planning and regular review.			
Have you taken any steps to agree shared aims and objectives with front-line staff?	Yes ☐ No ☐		
Does your team have clear workload targets that have been agreed by all agencies in the team?	Yes ☐ No ☐		

Structural issues - systems and management		If 'yes' how do you know this? What have you done?	If 'no' what action could you take?
Research tip: Integrated working models can unintentionally sideline participants, such as those who work part time, are seconded for short periods or are not co-located.			
Do clear systems and procedures exist to inform part-time team members about what has taken place in their absence?	Yes ☐ No ☐		
Research tip: Co-location can drive integrated practice; there is evidence that it enhances communication, learning and understanding of roles.			
Are staff co-located in shared buildings?	Yes ☐ No ☐		
Do any structures exist for communication with all stakeholders (eg a steering group)?	Yes ☐		

Research tip: Professionals in an integrated team are often juggling two identities; they need time and support to adapt. Different professionals may have very different service conditions; reducing these differences should enhance integrated practice.			
In your team, have all agencies made transparent efforts to minimise inequalities? (For example, these could be caused by different terms and conditions of service for team members employed by different agencies.)	Yes ☐ No ☐		

Now what? Think about celebrating what you have achieved in your integrated practice and how to build on those successes. This checklist may highlight particular actions your team should plan to take. Consider how you would focus your efforts to improve your integrated working.

Don't let this audit become an end in itself. Let it help you move forward. Action planning must follow. The results should give you a good indication of what you need to do to provide better conditions for integrated working. Use these results to help you formulate an action plan that both celebrates and builds on achievements and successes and addresses weaker areas.

TOOL 14

See Tool 14 Action plan

Adapted from Anning et al (2006) *Developing Multi-professional Teamwork for Integrated Children's Services.* Maidenhead: Open University Press

authority to make decisions about day-to-day team functions (as long as it is in accord with agreed targets and objectives)?	No		
Research tip: Integrated teams tend to be complex; lines of accountability can easily become more blurred than in traditional agencies with vertical management structures. This complexity should not be allowed to dilute clear lines of accountability, support and supervision.			
Is there clarity in your team about line management arrangements for all team members?	Yes No		
Do front-line practitioners have the authority to make decisions about day-to-day team functions (as long as it is in accord with agreed targets and objectives)?	Yes No		

continued on reverse

TOOL 5

Checklist: Ideological frameworks – sharing and redistributing knowledge, skills and beliefs

This checklist will help you decide where to focus your efforts to achieve effective integrated practice.

Ideological frameworks – sharing and redistributing knowledge, skills and beliefs		If 'yes' how do you know this? What have you done?	If 'no' what action could you take?
Research tip (Frost, 2005): Practitioners will develop new professional identities as part of the integrated setting, but will also want to maintain positive aspects of their existing professional identities. Managerial support is required to address these issues through training, supervision and time for reflection.			
Are different ways of working and professional skills respected within the team?	Yes ☐ No ☐		
Are different professional groups accorded equal respect within the team?	Yes ☐ No ☐		

Ideological frameworks – sharing and redistributing knowledge, skills and beliefs		If 'yes' how do you know this? What have you done?	If 'no' what action could you take?
Research tip: Integrated working is about improving the process and outcomes of working with service users. We have to take their views and experiences seriously.			
Does the team take account of service users' views about the way you work with them in partnership?	Yes ☐ No ☐		

Now what?

Don't let this audit become an end in itself. Let it help you move forward. Action planning must follow. The results should give you a good indication of what you need to do to provide better conditions for integrated practice. Use these results to help you formulate an action plan that both celebrates and builds on achievements and successes and addresses weaker areas.

See Tool 14
Action plan

Checklist: Ideological frameworks – sharing a[nd] redistributing knowledge, skills and beliefs

Adapted from Anning et al (2006) *Developing Multi-professional Teamwork for Integrated Children's Services* and Frost N (2005) *Professionalism, Partnership and Joined-up Thinking: a research review of front-line working with children and families.*

Research tip: Where integrated working is built, and where roles may become blurred, front-line staff require clear lines of accountability and appropriate professional support and supervisory arrangements.			
Is supervision of work attuned to the different needs of the individuals within the team and their various professional backgrounds?	Yes ☐ No ☐		
Research tip: Professionals working in integrated teams can learn from each other – a process that needs to be supported and facilitated.			
Does the team have any arrangement in place to encourage practitioners to share their different and common professional skills with each other?	Yes ☐ No ☐		

continued on reverse

TOOL 6

Checklist: Procedural influences – participation in developing new processes

This checklist will help you decide where to focus your efforts to achieve effective integrated practice.

Procedural influences – participation in developing new processes		If 'yes' how do you know this? What have you done?	If 'no' what action could you take?
Research tip (Frost, 2005): It is necessary to have detailed planning procedures to ensure that roles and responsibilities are clear and sustainable as integrated working develops.			
Has the integrated team developed new processes and procedures in order to meet its agreed objectives?	Yes ☐ No ☐		
Do staff in the team have to follow inappropriate agency-of-origin procedures where they are in conflict with agreed team objectives?	Yes ☐ No ☐		

Are there regular opportunities for whole-team discussion of client-focused activities?	Yes ☐ No ☐		
Do agencies in the integrated team continue to provide ongoing support for the professional development of their staff as well as supporting team development activities?	Yes ☐ No ☐		

Now what?

Don't let this audit become an end in itself. Let it help you move forward. Action planning must follow. The results should give you a good indication of what you need to do to provide better conditions for integrated practice. Use these results to help you formulate an action plan that both celebrates and builds on achievements and successes and addresses weaker areas.

Checklist: Procedural influences – participa in developing new processes

Adapted from Anning et al (2006) *Developing Multi-professional Teamwork for Integrated Children's Services* and Frost N (2005) *Professionalism, Partnership and Joined-up Thinking: a research review of front-line working with children and families.*

Research tip: Integrated practice is complex, difficult and challenging; staff will need time to reflect on, discuss and review their practice and related policies.			
Do opportunities exist for team members to have time away from the immediacy of delivering services in order to reflect on practice and develop new ways of working (eg team away days, joint team training events)?	Yes ☐ No ☐		
Research tip (Frost, 2005): It is necessary to have detailed planning procedures to ensure that roles and responsibilities are clear and sustainable as integrated working develops.			
Do you engage in joint client-focused activities such as shared assessment and/or consultation with families?	Yes ☐ No ☐		

continued on reverse

TOOL 7

Checklist: Interprofessional learning – through role change

This checklist will help you decide where to focus your efforts to achieve effective integrated practice.

Interprofessional learning - through role change		If 'yes' how do you know this? What have you done?	If 'no' what action could you take?
Research tip (Frost, 2005): Effective leadership is crucial. Effective leaders of integrated teams often have strong 'entrepreneurial' skills, enabling them to broker interagency agreements and operate across traditional divides to create new solutions.			
Does the integrated team have good and clear leadership?	Yes ☐ No ☐		
Research tip: One challenge of integrated working is that roles can easily become confused; effective integrated working should not imply that people become unclear about exactly what they do.			
Are roles within the team clear?	Yes ☐		

Interprofessional learning - through role change		If 'yes' how do you know this? What have you done?	If 'no' what action could you take?
Research tip: Staff may fear their expertise will be undermined by an emphasis on generalist working; in effective teams, their skills can be recognised and developed to the benefit of all.			
Do people in the team allow individual members to retain and develop their 'specialist' skills?	Yes ☐ No ☐		
Is the contribution of part-time team members acknowledged?	Yes ☐ No ☐		

Now what?

Checklist: Interprofessional learning – through role change

See Tool 14
Action plan

Adapted from Anning et al (2006) *Developing Multi-professional Teamwork for Integrated Children's Services* and Frost N (2005) *Professionalism, Partnership and Joined-up Thinking: a research review of front-line working with children and families.*

Research tip: Requirements of integration cannot erase the harsh reality of barriers related to status and hierarchies. Integrated working must recognise, celebrate and build on diversity and difference.			
Does the team always allow certain individuals or professional groups to dominate?	Yes ☐ No ☐		
Is the contribution of part-time team members acknowledged?	Yes ☐ No ☐		

continued on reverse

TOOL 8

Are we making a difference? Focus on outcomes

How do we know we are making a difference for the children and families we work with? Outcomes are the impact, effect or consequence of help received. They define what success looks like in your integrated team. A clear focus on improving outcomes for children and young people should be at the heart of integrated working.

The aim of this Tool is to assist you in translating the requirements of the Children Act 2004 into goals, and to check knowledge and progress against those goals. The intention is to encourage integrated teams to think about how they move from the general – the overarching national outcomes – to their application in the particular for integrated practice on the front line.

Work through the questions as a team to check how outcome-focused you are. As you go, use the space at the end to jot down ideas about what you might do to move outcomes more to centre stage.

Use this Tool to explore to what extent your multiagency team contributes to achieving the five outcomes for children and young people identified in the Children Act 2004?

Please score 1 – 5, where 1 equals 'little contribution' and 5 is 'high contribution'.

ECM Outcomes	Score (as above)	What is your evidence?
being healthy	1 2 3 4 5	
staying safe	1 2 3 4 5	
	1 2 3 4 5	

3. What performance indicators and information can be used to measure these outcomes, at either agency or partnership level?

4. How well is your integrated team doing on these indicators?

Room for improvement 1 2 3 4 5 Good (score)

5. Are the outcomes achieved the same for all the children and young people your team is engaged with? For example, do you know if there is a difference for children and young people who:

- are looked after
- have special educational needs/disabilities
- are from black and minority ethnic groups
- live in different areas
- are in different age bands
- have different types of needs?

6. How much do you ascribe these outcomes to integrated working?

very little 1 2 3 4 5 a lot (score)

7. What do you know about the long-term outcomes for the children and young people you work with?

Use this space to jot down ideas about what you might do to improve your team's understanding of outcomes.

Refer back to Tool 2 'Understanding your team' and see how everything fits together.

making a positive contribution	1 2 3 4 5	
achieving economic well-being	1 2 3 4 5	

1. What specific outcomes are your team seeking to achieve for the children and young people you are involved with? (Be sure to distinguish these outcomes from the actual services provided or the needs of your service users.)

2. How do you know that these are the specific outcomes that the children and young people, their families and the community themselves want?

continued on reverse

Adapted from Tool 16 in Atherton C, Barratt M and Hodson R (2005) *TEAMWISE Using Research Evidence: A practical guide for teams.* Dartington: **research in practice**

TOOL 9

Exploring attitudes and beliefs

How to use this Tool

Use this Tool to understand and reflect on your experience of integrated working and to reflect on difficult issues that may have surfaced. Look at the example given below and write your own account of a situation that has arisen. See if you, as a team, can reflect on the learning from the incident and identify specific issues for discussion. Use this scenario as a means of understanding and reflecting on your experiences of integrated practice.

But beware! Disagreements may emerge here. Make a note of these disagreements and seek support for resolving them. Set out some ground rules for this exercise before you start.

Think of an incident, episode or event (Anning, 2006) and take five or ten minutes to write it down.

Think about:

- What happened?
- When, where and who was involved?
- What was the history and build up to the incident?
- How did you respond?
- What did you do straight away and later?
- How was the team involved?
- What practitioners and agencies were involved?
- What did they do straight away and later?
- What did you learn from this incident?

Discuss

Conflict	Learning	Issues raised for discussion

Conflict

Learning

Issues raised for discussion

Exploring attitudes and beliefs

your incident

team began with a very effective leader who was a strong advocate for the project within the organisation. This key person was moved with no communication or agreement with partner agencies. This led to a loss of specialist skills, leadership and influence. Some team members felt the loss of this team member caused confusion with regard to roles and responsibilities within the team. A period of 're-consolidation' was needed before the team felt strong again.	it was crucial to take the issue up with senior managers and remind them of their responsibilities to integrated working. The leader's role had always been under threat because it had never been factored into the running costs. It was, and is, essential, whenever possible, to ensure that roles are financially secured, especially in respect of seconded staff where it is clear (for the purpose of continuity of service) that the post should be a permanent post.	• communication within the team • loss of specialist skills • clarity about roles and responsibilities • financial security for particular roles (Since being challenged, this particular agency has given careful consideration to any proposal to move staff. This has been a change for that agency's culture.)

example

continued on reverse

Incident quoted in the Development Group for the Change Project (2008)

TOOL 10

Common Core of Skills and Knowledge

The Common Core of Skills and Knowledge for the Children's Workforce sets out the basic skills and knowledge needed by people (including volunteers) whose work brings them into regular contact with children, young people and families. It will enable different professionals in teams to work together more effectively in the interests of the child.[1]

How to use this Tool

1. Without looking at the rest of this Tool, write down what skills and knowledge you think are needed to practice at a basic level in these six areas of expertise listed here.

1. Effective communication with children, young people and families	
Skills	*(eg listening and building empathy)* **1.** **2.** **3.**
Knowledge	*(eg how communication works)* **1.** **2.** **3.**

TOOL 10

Common Core of Skills and Knowledge

4. Supporting transitions	
Skills	1. 2.
Knowledge	1. 2.
5. Multiagency working	
Skills	1. 2.
Knowledge	1. 2. 3. 4.
6. Sharing information	

	2.
	3.
Knowledge	1.
	2.
	3.
	4.

Now look at the list overleaf (the Common Core of Skills and Knowledge for the Children's Workforce) and see what is common to your list.

Tips:

- Work in groups to identify common skills and knowledge among professionals.
- Highlight the similarities within practice while valuing different specialisms.

[1] Every Child Matters website www.everychildmatters.gov.uk/deliveringservices/commoncore

2. Child and young person development	
Skills	1. 2.
Knowledge	1. 2. 3. 4.
3. Safeguarding and promoting the welfare of the child	
Skills	1. 2. 3.
Knowledge	1. 2. 3.

[1] Every Child Matters website www.everychildmatters.gov.uk/deliveringservices/commoncore

	Understanding how babies, children and young people develop Being clear about your own job role Knowing how to reflect and improve	
3. Safeguarding and promoting the welfare of the child		
Skills	Relating, recognising and taking considered action Communicating, recording and reporting Personal skills	
Knowledge	Legal and procedural frameworks Wider context of services Self-knowledge	
4. Supporting transitions		
Skills	Identifying transitions Providing support	
Knowledge	How children and young people respond to change When and how to intervene	

	Awareness of complexities Awareness of laws and legislation	
	TOTAL	

How did you score out of 36?

Over time it is expected that everyone working with children, young people and families will be able to demonstrate a basic level of competence in the six areas of the Common Core. In the future, the Common Core will form part of qualifications for working with children, young people and families and it will act as a foundation for training and development programmes run by employers and training organisations.

Try and identify what your training needs might be in areas you may need to develop. Do this on two levels – for you personally, and for the members of the team as a whole.

TOOL 10

Common Core of Skills and Knowledge for the Children's Workforce

5. Multiagency working		Did you include this on your list?
Skills	Communication and teamwork Assertiveness	
Knowledge	Your role and remit Knowing how to make queries Procedures and working methods The law policies and procedures	
6. Sharing information		
Skills	Information handling Clear communication Engagement	
Knowledge	Importance of information sharing	

TOOL 10

Common Core of Skills and Knowledge for the Children's Workforce

The skills and knowledge needed for effective integrated practice are described under six main headings:

1. Effective communication with children, young people and families		Did you include this on your list?
Skills	Listening and building empathy Summarising and explaining Consultation and negotiation	
Knowledge	How communication works Confidentiality and ethics Sources of support Importance of respect	
2. Child and young person development		
Skills	Observation and judgement Empathy and understanding	